WHAT KIND OF CREATURES ARE WE?

COLUMBIA THEMES IN PHILOSOPHY

COLUMBIA THEMES IN PHILOSOPHY
Series Editor
Akeel Bilgami, Johnsonian Professor of Philosophy, Columbia University

Columbia Themes in Philosophy is a new series with a broad and accomodating thematic reach as well as an ecumenical approach to the outdated disjunction between analytic and European philosophy. It is committed to an examination of key themes in new and startling ways and to the exploration of new topics in philosophy.

Edward Said, *Humanism and Democratic Criticism*

Michael Dummet, *Truth and the Past*

John Searle, *Freedom and Neurobilogy: Reflections on Free Will, Language, and Political Power*

Daniel herwitz and Michael Kelley, eds., *Action, Art, History: Engagement with Arthur C. Danto*

Michael Dummet, *The Nature and Future of Philosophy*

Jean Bricmont and Julie Franck, eds., *Chomsky Notebook*

Mario De Caro and David Macarthur, eds., *Naturalism and Normativity*

Alan Montefiore, *A Philosophical retrospective: Facts, Values, and Jewish Identity*

Thom Brooks and Martha C. Nussbaum, eds., *Rawl's Political Liberalsim*

What Kind of CREATURES Are We?

NOAM CHOMSKY

Columbia University Press NEW YORK

COLUMBIA UNIVERSITY PRESS
Publishers Since 1893
NEW YORK   CHICHESTER, WEST SUSSEX
cup.columbia.edu

Library of Congress Cataloging-in-Publication Data

Chomsky, Noam, author.
    What kind of creatures are we? / Noam Chomsky.
        pages cm. — (Columbia Themes in Philosophy)
    Includes bibliographical references and index.
    ISBN 978-0-231-17596-8 (cloth : alk. paper)
    ISBN 978-0-231-54092-6 (e-book)
    1. Language and languages—Philosophy.   I. Title.
    P106.C46 2016
    401—dc23

                            2015021707

Columbia University Press books are printed on permanent and durable acid-free paper.
This book is printed on paper with recycled content.
Printed in the United States of America
c 10 9 8 7 6 5 4

COVER IMAGE: RICCARDO VECCHIO
COVER DESIGN: CHANG JAE LEE

CONTENTS

Akeel Bilgrami

THIS BOOK PRESENTS a lifetime of reflection by a scientist of language on the broader implications of his scientific work. The title of this volume, *What Kind of Creatures Are We?*, conveys just how broad the implications are meant to be. They cover an impressive range of fields: theoretical linguistics, cognitive science, philosophy of science, history of science, evolutionary biology, metaphysics, the theory of knowledge, the philosophy of language and mind, moral and political philosophy, and, even briefly, the ideal of human education.

Chapter 1 presents, with clarity and precision, Noam Chomsky' own basic ideas in theoretical linguistics and cognitive science (both fields in which he has played an absolutely central founding role), recording the progress achieved over the years but recording much more strenuously how tentatively those claims to progress must be made and how a very large amount of work remains to be done even in the most fundamental areas of study. Changes of mind over these years are also recorded, some of the most striking of which occurred only in the past decade or so.

The chapter begins by motivating the question its title announces, "What Is Language?" It behooves us to ask it because without being clear about what language is, not only will we not get the right answers to other questions about various specific aspects of language (perhaps cannot even correctly frame those specific questions), but we will not get close to investigating or even plausibly speculating about the biological basis and evolutionary origins of language.

A tradition that goes back to Galileo and Descartes recognized the most fundamental feature of language, which then got its most explicit articulation in Humboldt: "Language is quite peculiarly confronted by an unending and truly boundless domain, the essence of all that can be thought. It must therefore make infinite employment of finite means, and is able to do so, through the power which produces identity of language and thought."[1] Darwin, too, is cited as repeating this in a more elementary form in the context of evolutionary concerns about language: "The lower animals differ from man solely in his almost infinitely larger power of associating together the most diversified sounds and ideas." It is worth noting that there are three fundamental features observed here by Humboldt and Darwin. First, the claim to an infinite power residing in a finite base; second, the link of ideas with sound; and third, the link of language with thought. All of them are gathered in what Chomsky declares at the outset as the Basic Property of language: "[E]ach language provides an unbounded array of hierarchically structured expressions that receive interpretations at two interfaces, sensorimotor for externalization and conceptual-intentional for mental processes." The hierarchical-structural element speaks to the first feature; the sensorimotor interface, to the second feature; and the conceptual-intentional interface, to the third feature.

What will account for this Basic Property is a computational procedure. The philosophical significance of this is two-fold: a theory of language is necessarily a generative grammar, and the theory is necessarily about an object that individual human beings possess, internal to the individual subject and its mentality (i.e., intensional elements). It is not a theory about externalized utterances, nor is it, therefore, about a social phenomenon. The nomenclature to capture this latter distinction between what is individual/internal/intensional and what is externalized/social is I-language and E-language respectively. It is I-languages that alone can be the object of scientific study, not E-languages.[2] And although such study is eventually to be redeemed in a biological account, until that eventuality the science captures the phenomena at a level of abstraction from the biology and speaks at the cognitive level of the computational power that satisfies the Basic Property.[3]

A different, more general, task is to discover the shared underlying features of all I-languages, which is determined again by the biological properties with which human beings are endowed (a theme whose wider significance for cognition in general is discussed again in chapter 2). This more general task is undertaken with a view to discovering the biological endowment that determines what generative systems can serve as I-languages. In other words, what are the possible human languages?

Chomsky then points out that as soon as the study of generative grammars addressing the Basic Property of language was seriously undertaken, some surprising puzzles emerged, with far-reaching implications. One is the "structure dependence" of linguistic operations: in all constructions, in all languages, these operations invariably rely on structural distance rather than on the computationally far simpler notion of linear distance. Language learners know this automatically, without instruction. There is support for this from evidence from experimental neuroscience and psychology. The result follows from the assumption that the order is simply not available to the operations that generate the structured expressions that are interpreted at the conceptual-intentional interface, for thought and organization of action. That follows, in turn, from the very natural assumption that I-languages are generative systems based on the most elementary computational operation, which is order-free. These and numerous other considerations provide substantial evidence that linear order is ancillary to language, not involved in core syntax and semantics. The same is true of the various external arrangements of sign language, which is now known to be remarkably like spoken language in its structure, acquisition, use, and even neural representation. Presumably, these external properties reflect conditions imposed by the sensorimotor system. The option of using linear order does not even arise for the language learner. Linear order and other arrangements are relevant to what is heard—that is, externalized—not to what is thought, which is interior.

He then points out that these conclusions accord well with the little that is known about the origin of language. The sensorimotor system "appear[s] to have been in place long before language emerged," and there seems to be little specific adaptation for language. Cognitive properties of far deeper kinds than those possessed by apes, or presumably nonhuman hominins, are intrinsic to language. Apes have gestural systems adequate for signing and auditory systems adequate for perception of speech; but unlike human infants, they interpret speech as just noise, and even with extensive training cannot achieve even rudiments of human sign language. Aristotle said that language is "sound with meaning," but these considerations just outlined suggest to Chomsky that the priorities in the slogan may be reversed and language would be better understood as "meaning with sound." In case this comes off as Platonist (something that was zealously propagated by Jerrold Katz), it must be kept firmly in mind that for Chomsky, "meaning" here is intended as a thoroughly psychological (eventually biological) category and thus not at all reified in Platonist terms.

Such conclusions, in turn, fuel Chomsky's long-standing claim that language is not to be understood as it everywhere is among philosophers, anthropologists, and others—as in some defining way tied to communication. If externalization of language is secondary, and the tie of language to thought is primary, then communication cannot be central to any answer to the question this chapter asks: What is language? Indeed, as he says, there is reason to think that most of language/thought is not externalized at all. If one firmly understands that language is not designed by human beings but is part of their biological endowment, then, taking language as an object of study, whether scientific or philosophical, there might have to be considerable shift in our methodological approaches.

The quotation from Darwin that Chomsky cites with approval has it that what is fundamental about language is a "power of associating together the most diversified sounds and ideas." Except for the fact that, as we have mentioned, sound (along with other modes of externalization) has been demoted, Chomsky's own theoretical account of the Basic Property takes this point in Darwin for its word—though perhaps not the exact word, since "associating" is not exactly right in describing the central operation that the account posits. Associating happens, after all, even in classical conditioning (bell, food), and Chomsky has famously repudiated behaviorist accounts of language. Moreover, associations between two objects, as even nonbehaviorist psychologists understand association, may imply that the order of the objects is important in a way that the far greater weight put on the forms suited for semantic interpretation at the conceptual-intentional interface (rather than the sensorimotor interface) establishes it is not. So moving away from Darwin's misleading word "associating" for what Darwin himself wants to say, what Chomsky has in mind is to make central that we are unique in possessing the capacity to "put together" ideas and syntactic elements. And this fundamental conception of language is echoed in the theoretical account of the Basic Property, in which the crucial operation is given the name Merge, which can operate externally on two distinct objects to create another, or can operate internally from within one object to create another, yielding automatically the ubiquitous property of "displacement" (phrases heard in one place but understood also in a different place) in the form appropriate for complex semantic interpretation.

These are called External and Internal Merge, respectively, and respect for simplicity in scientific method, applicable in linguistics as anywhere else, dictates that we keep the basic operation down to this minimum and not proliferate operations in accounting for the computational power that grounds the

Basic Property. Working through some examples to present how language design is at its optimal if we stick to this methodological injunction, Chomsky presents changes in his own view, such as on the phenomenon of "displacement," which he once saw as an "imperfection," but now, if one correctly keeps to the simplest methodological assumptions as just mentioned, is something that is simply to be expected.

The chapter concludes with a bold attempt to exploit these last methodological points to bring two seemingly disparate questions together: What account shall we give of the Basic Property? How and when did language emerge? This confluence of simplicity of assumptions in accounting for the Basic Property and the accompanying claim of the optimal design of language may help to give substance to what is the most plausible hypothesis on the limited evidence we possess about the origins of language: that language emerged not gradually, but suddenly (and relatively recently). Such a sudden "great leap forward," it may now be speculated, was perhaps caused by a "slight rewiring of the brain [that] yielded Merge, naturally in its simplest form, providing the basis for unbounded and creative thought," hitherto unpossessed.

Chapter 2, "What Can We Understand?," consolidates some of these conclusions by first elaborating on another central theme in Chomsky's work: the limits of human cognition.

There is a locution we have all used frequently: "the scope and limits of . . ." Chomsky takes it very seriously and gives it a crucial twist in elaborating his understanding of our cognitive abilities. These abilities, which in their scope are wider and deeper than those of any other creature we know, are so partly *because* they are also subject to limits, limits owing to our nature or, as the title of the book suggests, the kinds of creatures we are—in particular, the fact that our cognitive abilities have a biological basis.

We implicitly came across this point in chapter 1, though it is restricted there to the human ability for language, in particular. The theoretical account of language presented there presupposed this notion of limits—that is, presupposed that we are genetically endowed with innate structures that afford us our unique capacity for language, structures that at the same time constrain what language is for us, what possible I-languages there are. It is for the characterization of these innate structures that the technical term "UG" is intended, and it is within the framework of the scope *and limits* set by this genetic endowment that language as a computational power is explained in the generative account summarized earlier.

What is true of language is just a special case of a perfectly general set of scopes and limits that come from the fact of being creatures with a biology. The idea seems to raise no controversy when it comes to physical ability: what makes us suited to walk limits us, so that we are not suited to slither like snakes.[4] Chomsky thinks that it is a prejudice to deny that what is obvious in the case of such physical abilities is not obvious (as the incessant controversies around innate ideas would suggest) in the case of cognitive abilities. To possess some cognitive abilities necessarily means that other cognitive abilities may be missing, cognitive abilities that other sorts of minded subjects could conceivably possess. It is only if we ignore the fact of our biology when we study human cognition that we would contrive to deny these limits. And chapter 2 proceeds to look at the

question of such limits on our cognitive abilities quite generally, beyond the specific domain of language, though returning
at various points to draw conclusions about language again.

It explores the methodological upshot of this idea of cognitive limits by first recalling a distinction that Chomsky made
almost five decades ago between "problems" and "mysteries."
Invoking Peirce's understanding of scientific method and scientific growth that appeals to the concept of abduction, which
puts *limits* on what count as "*admissible* hypotheses," he argues
that innate structures that are determined by our genetic endowment set limits to the questions that we can formulate.
The questions we can tractably formulate are called "problems," but given the limits within which their formulation is
so much as possible, there will be things that escape our cognitive powers; to the extent that we can even think them, we
will, given our current conceptual frameworks and knowledge,
find ourselves unable to formulate them in a way that a tractable form of scientific inquiry of them can be pursued. These
he calls "mysteries." The title of this book, *What Kind of Creatures Are We?*, is directly addressed by this, since other sorts of
creatures, with a different biological endowment from ours,
may be able to formulate problems that remain mysteries to
us. Thus for Chomsky, if not for Peirce (who, in speaking of admissible hypotheses, may have given less of a determining role
to the fact of our being biological creatures),[5] the distinction
between "problems" and "mysteries" is organism-relative.

It is a very important part of this methodological picture
that we should learn to relax with the fact of our cognitive
limits and the "mysteries" that they inevitably force us to

acknowledge. The final chapter in this volume, "The Mysteries of Nature," traverses vital moments in the history of science to draw this methodological lesson.

One crux moment is when Newton overturned the contact-mechanical assumptions of the early modern science that preceded him and posited a notion of gravity that undermined the earlier notions of matter, motion, and causality, which were scientific consolidations of our commonsense understanding (presumably determined by the cognitive limits of our biology) of the world of objects. Chomsky points out that with Newton, a new framework emerged in which—by the lights of those limits—something inconceivable was being proposed. Newton himself admitted to this inconceivability, even calling it an absurdity, and nobody since Newton has done anything to redeem things on just this score. Rather, the absurdity has simply been subsumed into our scientific picture of the world. Newton never let it deter him, constructing explanatory laws and ignoring the lack of a deeper underlying understanding that would, if we had it, make sense of what were, by these admissions on his (and others') part, described as an "occult" force. It was *sufficient* to construct intelligible theories of the world. And to do so, it was not necessary to find the world intelligible in the deeper sense that our cognitive limits frustrate.

Subsequent thinkers (Priestley, in particular, comes through as a most shrewd and comprehending commentator) made explicit this methodological outlook and drew consequences for issues in the philosophy of mind that vex philosophers today, but that, were they to take in what Priestley had to offer, might make them reconsider what they present as the mind-body problem, or "*the* hard problem" of consciousness. Philosophers have a tendency to stamp some issue as *uniquely* "hard" and rest complacently in that frustrated register. Chomsky appeals to precisely this history to show first of all that there is nothing unique about finding something "hard" in just this way. Thus, for instance, what the introduction of "gravity" did in physics was conceived to be just as hard in the aftermath of Newton, including by Newton himself.[6] The significance of this to the so-called mind-body problem is that it puts into doubt whether it can any longer—since Newton— even be formulated coherently. The initially anxiety-inducing introduction of something "mysterious" like "gravity" eventually became essential to our understanding of material bodies and their acting on each other without contact, and so it simply got incorporated into science—indeed, the new common sense of science. From this, we should, if anything, conclude philosophically that everything is immaterial, so nothing clear can remain of a mind-body problem. In a memorably eloquent reversal of Ryle's slogan, Chomsky says that far from the ghost having been sent to oblivion, the machine was discarded and the ghost remained intact. As for consciousness, the philosopher's tendency to require that much of our mentality be conscious, a tendency explicit in philosophers as different as Quine and Searle, is brought into question by looking at the operations of the rule-bound abilities of both language and vision. Chomsky feels particularly strongly about this, since even much of our conscious thought interacts with aspects of mind that are hidden from consciousness, and so to restrict oneself to what is conscious would hinder a scientific understanding of even the conscious mind.

Given his concern with a scientific account, he is concerned too to show that some ways of thinking about language, and thought more broadly, are not scientifically sound. There is, in particular, an extended discussion of the atomic elements of computation. Invoking points established in chapter 1, he points out that these are misleadingly described as "words" and as "lexical items" in the literature because—as they feed into the conceptual-intentional interface, which has been shown to be primary, in contrast with the sensorimotor interface—they are not constructed by the processes of externalization. Even more startling for philosophers is the claim that, except for some explicitly stipulative exceptions in mathematics and the sciences, they do not have any referential properties and are not to be thought of as bearing constitutive relations to mind-independent objects in the external world. I-language, which is the only scientifically accountable notion of language, thus, is thoroughly internal. This point is explored through a discussion of historical views, such as those of Aristotle and Hume, and by means of a discussion of examples of such atoms, ranging from the relatively concrete such as "house" and "Paris" to relatively abstract such as "person" and "thing." Reference or denotation is shown by these discussions to be too contextual to bear scientific study and should be seen as relevant to the use to which language is put rather than to a constitutive aspect of language itself. All this leads to a different taxonomy than is found among philosophers, relegating almost of all of what they have in mind by "semantics" to pragmatics.

These conclusions are relevant to the question of the origin of language. Animals' signals to one another are caused by direct links that they have to objects in the external world. There is no understanding them if one of these causal links is left out, whereas the burden of the preceding discussion was to show precisely that there are no such constitutive causal links to a mind-independent reality for the atoms of human computation. This gives further reason to conclude that the kind of creatures we are, possessed of the kind of powers for language and thought we possess, should get an evolutionary account of the sort presented in chapter 1 rather than what Chomsky, citing Lewontin in chapter 2, describes as the "storytelling" about gradual evolution from our creaturely ancestors, a mode of explanation that one would indulge in only if one does not pay enough prior and scientific attention to the nature of the phenotype being explained. It is storytelling partly also, as Lewontin is cited as saying, because of the "tough luck" of not having access to any evidence on which these explanations could be based. They are hidden from human cognitive access, another form of our limitation.

Thus limits on our cognition are inevitable for a variety of reasons, chief among which is the taking seriously of the sheer fact that we are biological creatures. Unlike Locke, Priestley, Hume, Russell, Peirce, and Lewontin, who are among the heroes of this chapter, Hilbert most explicitly ("There are absolutely no unsolvable problems") and much of contemporary philosophy more implicitly deny that there are mysteries, thereby denying a truism based on this sheer fact. What is fascinating is that Chomsky, having presented all this, takes an interesting combination of attitudes toward it. On the one hand, the very idea of cognitive limits that lands us human beings with "mysteries," which other sorts of subjects may find perfectly tractable, is a commitment to what philosophers call a *realist* metaphysics. As he says, "Given mysterian truisms, what is inconceivable to me is no criterion for what can exist." But on the other hand, taking his cue from Newton, his attitude, once this is acknowledged, is thoroughly *pragmatist*. Just because what we study, the world, may not be ultimately intelligible, does not mean that we should be inhibited from striving to produce intelligible scientific theories of the world. Even the concept of free human action, Chomsky says, which may go beyond any of the concepts we possess (crucially, determinacy and randomness) may one day be scientifically tractable, though we are far from anything like that understanding at present. This is quite different from the attitude of Kant, who declared freedom to be thinkable but never knowable. Like Peirce and before him Newton, and unlike Kant, Chomsky does not want his own mysterianism and his own insistence on the limits of our cognitive powers to place, as Peirce once put it, "roadblocks on the path to knowledge."

Chapter 3, "What Is the Common Good?," lifts the restriction on our natures, considered in terms of *individual* capacities (for language and cognition), and considers us as social creatures, seeking to explore what is the common good and which political and economic arrangements promote or thwart it.

The Enlightenment figures large in the pursuit of these questions, though what Chomsky has in mind by the Enlightenment is capacious, including the familiar "liberal" figures of Adam Smith[7] and Mill as well as those in a broadly Romantic tradition, such as Humboldt and Marx. And its interpretation is capacious, too, stressing not only the side of Smith that is often suppressed by most of his liberal and radical critics as well as his conservative devotees, but also the principles that allow the Enlightenment to be seen as a precursor of a later anarchist tradition in Europe as well as John Dewey in America.

The starting point of these inquiries is, in fact, individualist and has ties to the earlier chapters. Even within their biologically determined limits, the creative capacities that each individual possesses (and that were discussed in chapter 1 in the specific domain of language) are precisely the sort of thing whose full *development* makes individuals flower as subjects. The social question of the common good necessarily comes in when one asks what sorts of institutions hinder such development within the individual. Social frameworks such as capitalism that stress self-interest hinder rather than encourage the development of individual capacities. Both Smith's vivid excoriations of what the division of labor does to destroy our creative individuality and Dewey's harsh words on the shadow cast by corporate interests on just about every aspect of public and personal life are invoked to establish this. The tradition of anarchism (from Bakunin to Rudolph Rocker and the anarcho-syndicalism of the Spanish Civil War period) combines socialist ideas with the liberal principles of the classical Enlightenment to construct an ideal—of cooperative labor, workers' control of the workplace and the means of production, and a social life revolving around voluntary associations—that, if implemented, would sweep away the obstacles to the goal of human development that come from both free-market capitalism and Bolshevik tendencies to a "red bureaucracy." Dewey's ideas on education reveal how, by contrast with much of the contemporary practice found in educational institutions, the goal of human development can best be pursued from an early age.

There are touching descriptions of how many of these ideals were central to the activism of a wide range of grassroots movements—from the early radical parliamentary tradition in seventeenth-century England to the "factory girls" and artisans that Norman Ware wrote of in his study of industrial workers in the American tradition to the liberation theologians in the Catholic tradition of Central America. These long-standing democratic labor traditions are contrasted in some detail with a different understanding of democracy, in a tradition that begins in the United States with Madison's "aristocratic" strictures on who may govern and are updated in the vision of Walter Lippmann's ideas of democratic rule by the "expert," the American version of Leninist vanguardism, ensuring—as Chomsky makes clear with a glance at the results of polls on various important issues, such as health care—that what the people want is almost never what gets on the agenda of "democratic" politics. This latter understanding of democracy, of course, dominates the practice of societies and governments in much of the Western world, and Chomsky is keen to point out that even at its worst, it never lets up on the *claim* to be pursuing high-sounding ideals of the common good, showing how the common good is universal in a quite paradoxical way: it is preached as applying to all, even as it is everywhere violated by those who are said to be representing all but who mostly pursue the interests of a few.

Given the fundamental starting point in human creativity and the importance of its unhindered flowering, Chomsky's leaning toward anarchism is not surprising, and his way of putting the point has always been to declare, as he does in this lecture again: any form of coercion that hinders it can never be taken for granted. It needs a justification. All arrangements that have coercive power, including centrally the state, must always be justified. The default position is that they are not justified—until and unless they are. And given the contingency of the "shoals of capitalism" (his phrase) in all corners of the world, there is indeed a justification of a notion of the state that protects the vast numbers who are pushed to the margins of society (echoing Smith himself, who thought that only the state could alleviate the oppressive life that industrial capital forces on labor),[8] very different from the actual state in most societies, which, as Dewey is cited as saying, largely does the bidding of corporations and in doing so removes the socialist element from anarchism and allows only the libertarian element—as a result of which democracy becomes "neodemocracy" (to match "neoliberalism"), in which if one suffers in poverty it is because, as Hobbes might have put it, one has chosen to do so. Thus to turn one's back on this and to justify the state as offering protections for those who suffer under capitalism, far from contradicting anarchism, is a consistent application of its principles in historical contingencies, a point that Chomsky presents with a marvelous metaphor that he says he has borrowed from the Brazilian rural workers' movement and extended—the metaphor of an "iron cage" whose floors one tries to extend as one tries to reduce the coercive power of the state, even as the cage protects one from the destructive forces outside the cage, forces that render us weak and impoverished and alienated, to say nothing of rendering our planet uninhabitable.

I have tried, as best I can, to summarize a book whose intellectual complexity and power and whose breadth of knowledge and originality cannot possibly be captured in a summary—so, an exercise and duty that may not, in the end, aid the reader at all. But what I will say, without pause or condition, is that there was such pleasure and instruction in the exercise that I could do no better than ask the reader to study the book for herself—not only for the qualities I have just mentioned, but for its utter seriousness of purpose regarding the deepest questions in philosophy and science and, above all, its vast humanity.

WHAT KIND OF CREATURES ARE WE?

THE GENERAL QUESTION I would like to address in this book is an ancient one: What kind of creatures are we? I am not deluded enough to think I can provide a satisfactory answer, but it seems reasonable to believe that in some domains at least, particularly with regard to our cognitive nature, there are insights of some interest and significance, some new, and that it should be possible to clear away some of the obstacles that hamper further inquiry, including some widely accepted doctrines with foundations that are much less stable than often assumed.

I will consider three specific questions, increasingly obscure: What is language? What are the limits of human understanding (if any)? And what is the common good to which we should strive? I will begin with the first and will try to show how what may seem at first to be rather narrow and technical questions can, if pursued carefully, lead to some far-reaching conclusions that are significant in themselves and differ sharply from what is generally believed—and often regarded as fundamental—in the relevant disciplines: cognitive science in a broad sense, including linguistics, and philosophy of language and mind.

Throughout, I will be discussing what seem to me virtual truisms, but of an odd kind. They are generally rejected. That poses a dilemma, for me at least. And perhaps you too will be interested in resolving it.

Turning to language, it has been studied intensively and productively for 2,500 years, but with no clear answer to the question of what language is. I will mention later some of the major proposals. We might ask just how important it is to fill this gap. For the study of any aspect of language the answer should be clear. Only to the extent that there is an answer to this question, at least tacit, is it possible to proceed to investigate serious questions about language, among them acquisition and use, origin, language change, diversity and common properties, language in society, the internal mechanisms that implement the system, both the cognitive system itself and its various uses, distinct though related tasks. No biologist would propose an account of the development or evolution of the eye, for example, without telling us something fairly definite about what an eye is, and the same truisms hold of inquiries into language. Or should. Interestingly, that is not how the questions have generally been viewed, a matter to which I will return.

But there are much more fundamental reasons to try to determine clearly what language is, reasons that bear directly on the question of what kind of creatures we are. Darwin was not the first to conclude that "the lower animals differ from man solely in his almost infinitely larger power of associating together the most diversified sounds and ideas";[1] "almost infinite" is a traditional phrase to be interpreted today as actually infinite. But Darwin was the first to have expressed this traditional concept within the framework of an incipient account of human evolution.

A contemporary version is given by one of the leading scientists who studies human evolution, Ian Tattersall. In a recent review of the currently available scientific evidence, he observes that it was once believed that the evolutionary record would yield "early harbingers of our later selves. The reality, however, is otherwise, for it is becoming increasingly clear that the acquisition of the uniquely modern [human] sensibility was instead an abrupt and recent event. . . . And the expression of this new sensibility was almost certainly crucially abetted by the invention of what is perhaps the single most remarkable thing about our modern selves: language."[2] If so, then an answer to the question "What is language?" matters greatly to anyone concerned with understanding our modern selves.

Tattersall dates the abrupt and sudden event as probably lying somewhere within the very narrow window of 50,000 to 100,000 years ago. The exact dates are unclear, and not relevant to our concerns here, but the abruptness of the emergence is. I will return to the vast and burgeoning literature of speculation on the topic, which generally adopts a very different stance.

If Tattersall's account is basically accurate, as the very limited empirical evidence indicates, then what emerged in the narrow window was an infinite power of "associating the most diversified sound and ideas," in Darwin's words. That infinite power evidently resides in a finite brain. The concept of finite systems with infinite power was well understood by the mid-twentieth century. That made it possible to provide a clear formulation of what I think we should recognize to be the most basic property of language, which I will refer to just as the Basic Property: each language provides an unbounded array of hierarchically structured expressions that receive interpretations at two interfaces, sensorimotor for externalization and conceptual-intentional for mental processes. That allows a substantive formulation of Darwin's infinite power or, going back much farther, of Aristotle's classic dictum that language is sound with meaning—though work of recent years shows that sound is too narrow, and there is good reason, to which I will return, to think that the classic formulation is misleading in important ways.

At the very least, then, each language incorporates a computational procedure satisfying the Basic Property. Therefore a theory of the language is by definition a generative grammar, and each language is what is called in technical terms an I-language—"I" standing for internal, individual, and intensional: we are interested in the discovering the actual computational procedure, not some set of objects it enumerates, what it "strongly generates" in technical terms, loosely analogous to the proofs generated by an axiom system.

There is also a notion "weak generation"—the set of expressions generated, analogous to the set of theorems generated. There is also a notion "E-language," standing for external language, which many—not me—identify with a corpus of data, or with some infinite set that is weakly generated.[3] Philosophers, linguists, and cognitive and computer scientists have often understood language to be what is weakly generated. It is not clear that the notion weak generation is even definable for human language. At best it is derivative from the more fundamental notion of I-language. These are matters extensively discussed in the 1950s, though not properly assimilated, I believe.[4]

I will restrict attention here to I-language, a biological property of humans, some subcomponent of (mostly) the brain, an organ of the mind/brain in the loose sense in which the term "organ" is used in biology. I take the mind here to be the brain viewed at a certain level of abstraction. The approach is sometimes called the biolinguistic framework. It is regarded as controversial but without grounds, in my opinion.

In earlier years, the Basic Property resisted clear formulation. Taking some of the classics, for Ferdinand de Saussure, language (in the relevant sense) is a storehouse of word images in the minds of members of a community, which "exists only by virtue of a sort of contract signed by the members of a community." For Leonard Bloomfield, language is an array of habits to respond to situations with conventional speech sounds and to respond to these sounds with actions. Elsewhere, Bloomfield defined language as "the totality of utterances made in a speech community"—something like William Dwight Whitney's earlier conception of language as "the body of uttered and audible signs by which in human society thought is principally expressed," thus "audible signs for thought"—though this a somewhat different conception in ways to which I will return. Edward Sapir defined language as "a purely human and non-instinctive method of communicating ideas, emotions, and desires by means of a system of voluntarily produced symbols."[5]

With such conceptions it is not unnatural to follow what Martin Joos called the Boasian tradition, holding that languages can differ arbitrarily and that each new one must be studied without preconceptions.[6] Accordingly, linguistic theory consists of analytic procedures to reduce a corpus to organized form, basically techniques of segmentation and classification. The most sophisticated development of this conception was Zellig Harris's *Methods*.[7] A contemporary version is that linguistic theory is a system of methods for processing expressions.[8]

In earlier years, it was understandable that the question "What is language?" received only such indefinite answers as the ones mentioned, ignoring the Basic Property. It is, however, surprising to find that similar answers remain current in contemporary cognitive science. Not untypical is a current study on evolution of language, where the authors open by writing that "we understand language as the full suite of abilities to map sound to meaning, including the infrastructure that supports it,"[9] basically a reiteration of Aristotle's dictum, and too vague to ground further inquiry. Again, no biologist would study evolution of the visual system assuming no more about the phenotype than that it provides the full suite of abilities to map stimuli to percepts along with whatever supports it.

Much earlier, at the origins of modern science, there were hints at a picture somewhat similar to Darwin's and Whitney's. Galileo wondered at the "sublimity of mind" of the person who "dreamed of finding means to communicate his deepest thoughts to any other person . . . by the different arrangements of twenty characters upon a page," an achievement "surpassing all stupendous inventions," even those of "a Michelangelo, a Raphael, or a Titian."[10] The same recognition, and the deeper concern for the creative character of the normal use of language, was soon to become a core element of Cartesian science-philosophy, in fact a primary criterion for the existence of mind as a separate substance. Quite reasonably, that led to efforts to devise tests to determine whether another creature has a mind like ours, notably by Géraud de Cordemoy.[11] These were somewhat similar to the "Turing test," though quite differently conceived. De Cordemoy's experiments were like a litmus test for acidity, an attempt to draw conclusions about the real world. Turing's imitation game, as he made clear, had no such ambitions.

These important questions aside, there is no reason today to doubt the fundamental Cartesian insight that use of language has a creative character: it is typically innovative without bounds, appropriate to circumstances but not caused by them—a crucial distinction—and can engender thoughts in others that they recognize they could have expressed themselves. We may be "incited or inclined" by circumstances and internal conditions to speak in certain ways, not others, but we are not "compelled" to do so, as Descartes's successors put it. We should also bear in mind that Wilhelm von Humboldt's now oft-quoted aphorism that language involves infinite use of finite means refers to *use*. More fully, he wrote that "language is quite peculiarly confronted by an unending and truly boundless domain, the essence of all that can be thought. It must therefore make infinite employment of finite means, and is able to do so, through the power which produces identity of language and thought."[12] He thus placed himself in the tradition of Galileo and others who associated language closely with thought, though going well beyond, while formulating one version of a traditional conception of language as "the single most remarkable thing about our modern selves," in Tattersall's recent phrase.

There has been great progress in understanding the finite means that make possible infinite use of language, but the latter remains largely a mystery despite significant progress in understanding conventions that guide appropriate use, a much narrower question. How deep a mystery is a good question, to which I will return in chapter 2.

A century ago, Otto Jespersen raised the question of how the structures of language "come into existence in the mind of a speaker" on the basis of finite experience, yielding a "notion of structure" that is "definite enough to guide him in framing sentences of his own," crucially "free expressions" that are typically new to speaker and hearer.[13] The task of the linguist, then, is to discover these mechanisms and how they arise in the mind, and to go beyond to unearth "the great principles underlying the grammars of all languages," and by unearthing them to gain "a deeper insight into the innermost nature of human language and of human thought"—ideas that sound much less strange today than they did during the structuralist/behavioral science era that came to dominate much of the field, marginalizing Jespersen's concerns and the tradition from which they derived.

Reformulating Jespersen's program, the primary task is to investigate the true nature of the interfaces and the generative procedures that relate them in various I-languages, and to determine how they arise in the mind and are used, the primary focus of concern naturally being "free expressions." And to go beyond to unearth the shared biological properties that determine the nature of I-languages accessible to humans, the topic of UG, universal grammar, in the contemporary version of Jespersen's "great principles underlying the grammars of all languages," now reframed as a question of the genetic endowment that yields the unique human language capacity and its specific instantiations in I-languages.

The mid-twentieth-century shift of perspective to generative grammar within the biolinguistic framework opened the way to much more far-reaching inquiry into language itself and language-related topics. The range of empirical materials available from languages of the widest typological variety has enormously expanded, and they are studied at a level of depth that could not have been imagined sixty years ago. The shift also greatly enriched the variety of evidence that bears on the study of each individual language to include acquisition, neuroscience, dissociations, and much else, and also what is learned from the study of other languages, on the well-confirmed assumption that the capacity for language relies on shared biological endowment.

As soon as the earliest attempts were made to construct explicit generative grammars sixty years ago, many puzzling phenomena were discovered, which had not been noticed as long as the Basic Property was not clearly formulated and addressed and syntax was just considered "use of words" determined by convention and analogy. This is somewhat reminiscent of the early stages of modern science. For millennia, scientists had been satisfied with simple explanations for familiar phenomena: rocks fall and steam rises because they are seeking their natural place; objects interact because of sympathies and antipathies; we perceive a triangle because its shape flits through the air and implants itself in our brains, and so on. When

Galileo and others allowed themselves to be puzzled about the phenomena of nature, modern science began—and it was quickly discovered that many of our beliefs are senseless and our intuitions often wrong. Willingness to be puzzled is a valuable trait to cultivate, from childhood to advanced inquiry.

One puzzle about language that came to light sixty years ago, and remains alive and I think highly significant in its import, has to do with a simple but curious fact. Consider the sentence "instinctively, eagles that fly swim." The adverb "instinctively" is associated with a verb, but it is "swim," not "fly." There is no problem with the thought that eagles that instinctively fly swim, but it cannot be expressed this way. Similarly the question "Can eagles that fly swim?" is about ability to swim, not to fly.

What is puzzling is that the association of the clause-initial elements "instinctively" and "can" to the verb is remote and based on structural properties, rather than proximal and based solely on linear properties, a far simpler computational operation, and one that would be optimal for processing language. Language makes use of a property of minimal structural distance, never using the much simpler operation of minimal linear distance; in this and numerous other cases, ease of processing is ignored in the design of language. In technical terms, the rules are invariably *structure-dependent*, ignoring linear order. The puzzle is why this should be so—not just for English but for every language, not just for these constructions but for all others as well, over a wide range.

There is a simple and plausible explanation for the fact that the child reflexively knows the right answer in such cases as these, even though evidence is slight or nonexistent: linear order is simply not available to the language learner confronted with such examples, who is guided by a deep principle that restricts search to minimal structural distance, barring the far simpler operation of minimal linear distance. I know of no other explanation. And this proposal of course at once calls for further explanation: Why is this so? What is it about the genetically determined character of language—UG—that imposes this particular condition?

The principle of minimal distance is extensively employed in language design, presumably one case of a more general principle, call it Minimal Computation, which is in turn presumably an instance of a far more general property of the organic world or even beyond. There must however be some special property of language design that restricts Minimal Computation to structural rather than linear distance, despite the far greater simplicity of the latter for computation and processing.

There is independent evidence from other sources, including the neurosciences, supporting the same conclusion. A research group in Milan studied brain activity of subjects presented with two types of stimuli: invented languages satisfying UG and others not conforming to UG; in the latter case, for example, a rule for negation that places the negative element after the third word, a far simpler computational operation than the rules for negation in human language. They found that in the case of conformity to UG, there is normal activation in the language areas, though not when linear order is used.[14] In that case, the task is interpreted as a nonlinguistic puzzle, so brain activity indicates. Work by Neil Smith and Ianthi-Maria Tsimpli with a cognitively impaired but linguistically gifted subject reached similar conclusions—but, interestingly, found that normals as well were unable to deal with the violations of UG using linear order. As Smith concludes: "the linguistic format of the experiment appeared to inhibit them from making the appropriate structure-independent generalization, even though they could work out comparable problems in a nonlinguistic environment with ease."[15]

There is a small industry in computational cognitive science attempting to show that these properties of language can be learned by statistical analysis of Big Data. This is, in fact, one of the very few significant properties of language that has been seriously addressed at all in these terms. Every attempt that is clear enough to be investigated has been shown to fail, irremediably.[16] But more significantly, the efforts are beside the point in the first place. If they were to succeed, which is a virtual impossibility, they would leave untouched the original and only serious question: *Why* does language invariably use the complex computational property of minimal structural distance in the relevant cases, while always disregarding the far simpler option of minimal linear distance? Failure to grasp this point is an illustration of the lack of willingness to be puzzled that I mentioned earlier, the first step in serious scientific inquiry, as recognized in the hard sciences at least since Galileo.

A broader thesis is that linear order is never available for computation in the core parts of language involving syntax-semantics. Linear order, then, is a peripheral part of language, a reflex of properties of the sensorimotor system, which requires it: we cannot speak in parallel, or produce structures, but only strings of words. The sensorimotor system is not specifically adapted to language in fundamental respects: the parts essential for externalization and perception appear to have been in place long before language emerged. There is evidence that the auditory system of chimpanzees might be fairly well adapted for human speech,[17] though apes cannot even take the first step in language acquisition, extracting language-relevant data from the "blooming, buzzing confusion" surrounding them, as human infants do at once, reflexively, not a slight achievement. And though capacity to control the vocal tract for speech appears to be human-specific, that fact cannot bear too much weight given that production of human language is modality-independent, as recent work on sign language has established, and there is little reason to doubt that apes have adequate gestural capacities. Evidently much deeper cognitive properties are involved in language acquisition and design.

Though the matter is not settled, there is considerable evidence that the broader thesis may in fact be correct: fundamental language design ignores order and other external arrangements. In particular, semantic interpretation in core cases depends on hierarchy, not the order found in the externalized forms. If so, then the Basic Property is not exactly as I formulated it before, and as it is formulated in recent literature—papers of mine, too. Rather, the Basic Property is generation of an unbounded array of hierarchically structured expressions mapping to the conceptual-intentional interface, providing a kind of "language of thought"—and quite possibly the only such LOT, though interesting questions arise here. Interesting and important questions also arise about the status and character of this mapping, which I will put aside.

If this line of reasoning is generally correct, then there is good reason to return to a traditional conception of language as "an instrument of thought," and to revise Aristotle's dictum accordingly; language is not sound with meaning but meaning with sound—more generally, with some form of externalization, typically sound though other modalities are readily available: work of the past generation on sign has shown remarkable similarities to spoken language in structure, acquisition, and neural representation, though of course the mode of externalization is quite different.

It is worth noting that externalization is rarely used. Most use of language use by far is never externalized. It is a kind of internal dialogue, and the limited research on the topic, going back to some observations of Lev Vygotsky's,[18] conforms to what introspection suggests—at least mine: what reaches consciousness is scattered fragments. Sometimes, full-formed expressions instantly appear internally, too quickly for articulators to be involved, or probably even instructions to them. This is an interesting topic that has been barely explored, but could be subjected to inquiry, and has many ramifications.

The latter issue aside, investigation of the design of language gives good reason to take seriously a traditional conception of language as essentially an instrument of thought. Externalization then would be an ancillary process, its properties a reflex of the largely or completely independent sensorimotor system. Further investigation supports this conclusion. It follows that processing is a peripheral aspect of language, and that particular uses of language that depend on externalization, among them communication, are even more peripheral, contrary to virtual dogma that has no serious support. It would also follow that the extensive speculation about language evolution in recent years is on the wrong track, with its focus on communication.

It is, indeed, virtual dogma that the function of language is communication. A typical formulation of the idea is the following: "It is important that in a community of language users that words be used with the same meaning. If this condition is met it facilitates the chief end of language which is communication. If one fails to use words with the meaning that most people attach to them, one will fail to communicate effectively with others. Thus one would defeat the main purpose of language."[19]

It is, in the first place, odd to think that language has a purpose. Languages are not tools that humans design but biological objects, like the visual or immune or digestive system. Such organs are sometimes said to have functions, to be *for* some purpose. But that notion too is far from clear. Take the spine. Is its function to hold us up, to protect nerves, to produce blood cells, to store calcium, or all of the above? Similar questions arise when we ask about the function and design of language. Here evolutionary considerations are commonly introduced, but these are far from trivial; for the spine as well. For language, the various speculations about evolution typically turn to the kinds of communication systems found throughout the animal kingdom, but that is just again a reflection of the modern dogma and is likely to be a blind alley, for reasons already mentioned and to which I will return.

Furthermore, even insofar as language is used for communication, there is no need for meanings to be shared (or sounds, or structures). Communication is not a yes-or-no but rather a more-or-less affair. If similarities are not sufficient, communication fails to some degree, as in normal life.

Even if the term "communication" is largely deprived of substantive meaning and used as a cover term for social interaction of various kinds, it remains a minor part of actual language use, for whatever that observation is worth.

In brief, there is no basis for the standard dogma, and there is by now quite significant evidence that it is simply false. Doubtless language is sometimes used for communication, as is style of dress, facial expression and stance, and much else. But fundamental properties of language design indicate that a rich tradition is correct in regarding language as essentially an instrument of thought, even if we do not go as far as Humboldt in identifying the two.

The conclusion becomes even more solidly entrenched if we consider the Basic Property more closely. Naturally we seek the simplest account of the Basic Property, the theory with fewest arbitrary stipulations—each of which is, furthermore, a barrier to some eventual account of origin of language. And we ask how far this resort to standard scientific method will carry us.

The simplest computational operation, embedded in some manner in every relevant computational procedure, takes objects X and Y already constructed and forms a new object Z. Call it *Merge*. The principle of Minimal Computation dictates that neither X nor Y is modified by Merge, and that they appear in Z unordered. Hence Merge(X,Y) = {X,Y}. That does not of course mean that the brain contains sets, as some current misinterpretations claim, but rather that whatever is going on in the brain has properties that can properly be characterized in these terms—just as we don't expect to find the Kekulé diagram for benzene in a test tube.

Note that if language really does conform to the principle of Minimal Computation in this respect, we have a far-reaching answer to the puzzle of why linear order is only an ancillary property of language, apparently not available for core syntactic and semantic computations: language design is perfect in this regard (and again we may ask why). Looking further, evidence mounts in support of this conclusion.

Suppose X and Y are merged, and neither is part of the other, as in combining *read* and *that book* to form the syntactic object corresponding to "read that book." Call that case *External Merge*. Suppose that one is part of the other, as in combining Y = *which book* and X = *John read which book* to form *which book John read which book*, which surfaces as "which book did John read" by further operations to which I will return. That is an example of the ubiquitous phenomenon of displacement in natural language: phrases are heard in one place but interpreted both there and in another place, so that the sentence is understood as "for which book x, John read the book x." In this case, the result of Merge of X and Y is again {X, Y}, but with two *copies* of Y (= *which book*), one the original one remaining in X, the other the displaced copy merged with X. Call that *Internal Merge*.

It is important to avoid a common misinterpretation, found in the professional literature as well. There is no operation *Copy* or *Remerge*. Internal Merge happens to generate two copies, but that is the outcome of Merge under the principle of Minimal Computation, which keeps Merge in its simplest form, not tampering with either of the elements Merged. New notions of Copy or Remerge not only are superfluous; they also cause considerable difficulties unless sharply constrained to apply under the highly specific conditions of Internal Merge, which are met automatically under the simplest notion of Merge.

External and Internal Merge are the only two possible cases of binary Merge. Both come free if we formulate Merge in the optimal way, applying to any two syntactic objects that have already been constructed, with no further conditions. It would require stipulation to bar either of the two cases of Merge, or to complicate either of them. That is an important fact. For many years it was assumed—by me, too—that displacement is a kind of "imperfection" of language, a strange property that has to be explained away by some more complex devices and assumptions about UG. But that turns out to be incorrect. Displacement is what we should expect on the simplest assumptions. It would be an imperfection if it were lacking. It is sometimes suggested that External Merge is somehow simpler and should have priority in design or evolution. There is no basis for that belief. If anything, one could argue that Internal Merge is simpler since it involves vastly less search of the workspace for computation—not that one should pay much attention to that.

Another important fact is that Internal Merge in its simplest form—satisfying the overarching principle of Minimal Computation—commonly yields the structure appropriate for semantic interpretation, as just illustrated in the simple case of "which book did John read." However, these are the wrong structures for the sensorimotor system: universally in language, only the structurally most prominent copy is pronounced, as in this case: the lower copy is deleted. There is a revealing class of exceptions that in fact support the general thesis, but I will put that aside.[20]

Deletion of copies follows from another uncontroversial application of Minimal Computation: compute and articulate as little as possible. The result is that the articulated sentences have *gaps*. The hearer has to figure out where the missing element is. As well-known in the study of perception and parsing, that yields difficult problems for language processing, so-called *filler-gap* problems. In this very broad class of cases too, language design favors minimal computation, disregarding the complications in the processing and use of language.

Notice that any linguistic theory that replaces Internal Merge by other mechanisms has a double burden of proof to meet: it is necessary to justify the stipulation barring Internal Merge and also the new mechanisms intended to account for displacement—in fact, displacement with copies, generally the right forms for semantic interpretation.

The same conclusions hold in more complex cases. Consider, for example, the sentence "[which of his pictures] did they persuade the museum that [[every painter] likes best]?" It is derived by Internal Merge from the underlying structure "[which of his pictures] did they persuade the museum that [[every painter] likes [which of his pictures] best]?," formed directly by Internal Merge, with displacement and two copies. The pronounced phrase "which of his pictures" is understood to be the object of "likes," in the position of the gap, analogous to "one of his pictures" in "they persuaded the museum that [[every painter] likes [one of his pictures] best]." And that is just the interpretation that the underlying structure with the two copies provides.

Furthermore, the quantifier-variable relationship between *every* and *his* carries over in "[which of his pictures] did they persuade the museum that [[every painter] likes best]?" The answer can be "his first one"—different for every painter, as in one interpretation of "they persuaded the museum that [[every painter] likes [one of his pictures] best]." In contrast, no such answer is possible for the structurally similar expression "[which of his pictures] persuaded the museum that [[every painter] likes flowers]?," in which case "his pictures" does not fall within the scope of "every painter." Evidently, it is the unpronounced copy that provides the structure required for quantifier-variable binding as well as for the verb-object interpretation. The results once again follow straightforwardly from Internal Merge and copy deletion under externalization. There are many similar examples—along with interesting problems as complexity mounts.

Just as in the simpler cases, like "instinctively, eagles that fly swim," it is inconceivable that some form of data processing yields these outcomes. Relevant data are not available to the language learner. The results must therefore derive "from the original hand of nature," in Hume's phrase—in our terms, from genetic endowment, specifically the architecture of language as determined by UG in interaction with such general principles as Minimal Computation. In ways like these we can derive quite far-reaching and firm conclusions about the nature of UG.

One commonly reads claims in the literature that UG has been refuted, or does not exist. But this must be a misunderstanding. To deny the existence of UG—that is, of a biological endowment underlying the capacity for language—would be to hold that it is a miracle that humans have language but other organisms do not. The reference in these claims is presumably not to UG, however; rather, to descriptive generalizations—Joseph Greenberg's very important proposals on language universals, for example. For example, in an introduction to the new edition of Quine's *Word and Object*,[21] Patricia Churchland, with an irrelevant citation, writes that "linguistic universals, long the darlings of theorists, took a drubbing as one by one they fell to the disconfirming data of field linguists." Presumably she takes this to be confirmation of Quine's view that "timely reflection on method and evidence should tend to stifle much of the talk of linguistic universals," meaning generalizations about language. In reality, it is field linguists who have discovered and confirmed not only the generally valid and quite important generalizations but also the invariant properties of UG. The term "field linguists" means linguists concerned with data, whether they are working in the Amazon jungle, or in their offices in Belem, or in New York.

The fragment of truth in such observations is that generalizations are likely to have exceptions, which can be quite valuable as a stimulus to inquiry—for example, the exceptions to deletion of copies, which I just mentioned. That is a common experience in the sciences. The discovery of perturbations in the orbit of Uranus did not lead to the abandonment of Newton's principles and Kepler's laws, or to the broader conclusion that there are no physical laws, but to the postulation—later discovery—of another planet, Neptune. Exceptions to largely valid descriptive generalizations play a similar role quite generally in the sciences and have done so repeatedly in the study of language.

There is, then, persuasive and quite far-reaching evidence that if language is optimally designed, it will provide structures appropriate for semantic interpretation but that yield difficulties for perception and language processing (hence communication). There are many other illustrations. Take, say, passivization. It has been argued that passivization supports the belief that language is well designed for communication. Thus in the sentence "the boys took the books," if we wish to foreground "the books," the passive operation allows us to do so by saying "the books were taken by the boys." In fact, the conclusion is the opposite. The design of language, following from Minimal Computation, regularly bars this option. Suppose in the sentence "the boys took the books from the library" we wish to foreground "the library," yielding "the library was taken the books from by the boys." That's barred by language design, yet another barrier to communication.

The interesting cases are those in which there is a direct conflict between computational and communicative efficiency. In every known case, the former prevails; ease of communication is sacrificed. Many such cases are familiar, among them structural ambiguities and "garden path sentences" such as "the horse raced past the barn fell," interpreted as ungrammatical on first presentation. Another case of particular interest is so-called *islands*—constructions in which extraction (Internal Merge) is barred—insofar as these can be given principled explanations invoking computational efficiency. An illustration is the questions associated with the expression "they asked if the mechanics fixed the cars." We can ask "how many cars," yielding "how many cars did they ask if the mechanics fixed?" Or we can ask "how many mechanics," yielding "how many mechanics did they ask if fixed the cars?" The two interrogatives differ sharply in status: asking "how many mechanics" is a fine thought, but it has to be expressed by some circumlocution, again impeding communication; technically an ECP violation. Here, too, there appear to be counterexamples, in Italian for example. Recognition of these led to discoveries about the nature of null subject languages by Luigi Rizzi,[22] reinforcing the ECP principle, again illustrating the value of proposed generalizations and apparent exceptions.

There are many similar cases. Insofar as they are understood, the structures result from free functioning of the simplest rules, yielding difficulties for perception and language processing. Again, where ease of processing and communicative efficiency conflict with computational efficiency in language design, in every known case the former are sacrificed. That lends further support to the view of language as an instrument of thought, in interesting respects perfectly designed, with externalization an ancillary process, hence a fortiori communication and other uses of externalized language. As is often the case, what is actually observed gives quite a misleading picture of the principles that underlie it. The essential art of science is reduction of "complex visibles to simple invisibles," as Nobel laureate in chemistry Jean Baptiste Perrin put the matter.

To bring out more clearly just what is at stake, let us reverse the argument outlined here, putting it in a more principled way. We begin with the Basic Property of language and ask what the optimal computational system would be that captures it, adopting normal scientific method. The answer is *Merge* in its simplest form, with its two variants, External and Internal Merge, the latter yielding the "copy theory of movement." In a wide and important range of cases, that yields forms appropriate for semantic interpretation at the conceptual-intentional interface, forms which lack order or other arrangements. An ancillary process of externalization then converts the internally generated objects to a form adapted to the sensorimotor system, with arrangements that vary depending on the sensory modality for externalization. Externalization, too, is subject to Minimal Computation, so that copies are erased, yielding difficulties for language processing and use (including the special case of communication). A fallout of the optimal assumptions is that rules are invariably structure-dependent, resolving the puzzle discussed at the outset and others like it.

A broader research project—in recent years called *the minimalist program*—is to begin with the optimal assumption—the so-called *strong minimalist thesis*, SMT—and to ask how far it can be sustained in the face of the observed complexities and variety of the languages of the world. Where a gap is found, the task will be to see whether the data can be reinterpreted, or principles of optimal computation can be revised, so as to solve the puzzles within the framework of SMT, thus producing some support, in an interesting and unexpected domain, for Galileo's precept that nature is simple, and it is the task of the scientist to prove it. The task is of course a challenging one. It is fair to say, I think, that it seems a good deal more realistic today than it did only a few years ago, though enormous problems of course remain.

All of this raises at once a further question: Why should language be optimally designed, insofar as the SMT holds? This question that leads us to consideration of the origin of language. The SMT hypothesis fits well with the very limited evidence we have about the emergence of language, apparently quite recently and suddenly in the evolutionary time scale, as Tattersall discussed. A fair guess today—and one that opens rich avenues of research and inquiry—is that some slight rewiring of the brain yielded Merge, naturally in its simplest form, providing the basis for unbounded and creative thought, the "great leap forward" revealed in the archaeological record, and the remarkable differences separating modern humans from their predecessors and the rest of the animal kingdom. Insofar as the surmise is sustainable, we would have an answer to questions about apparent optimal design of language: that is what would be expected under the postulated circumstances, with no selectional or other pressures operating, so the emerging system should just follow laws of nature, in this case the principles of Minimal Computation—rather the way a snowflake forms.

These remarks only scratch the surface. Perhaps they can serve to illustrate why the answer to the question "What is Language?" matters a lot, and also to illustrate how close attention to this fundamental question can yield conclusions with many ramifications for the study of what kind of creature humans are.

IN CHAPTER 1, I discussed the question "What is language?" and considered what we can learn about the kind of creatures we are from close inquiry into this distinctive human possession. Quite a lot, I believe and tried to suggest and illustrate. In this chapter, I would like to move on to questions about our cognitive capacities more generally, and specifically, how they enter into the scope and limits of our understanding.

There is a concept called "the new mysterianism," coined by Owen Flanagan, who defined it as "a postmodern position designed to drive a railroad spike through the heart of scientism" by holding that consciousness may never be completely explained.[1] The term has been extended to broader questions about the scope and nature of explanations accessible to human intelligence. I will use the term in the broader sense, which seems to me the more significant one.

I am cited as one of the culprits responsible for this strange postmodern heresy, though I would prefer a different name: truism. That is what I thought forty years ago in proposing a distinction between *problems*, which fall within our cognitive capacities, and *mysteries*, which do not.[2] In terms I borrowed from Charles Sanders Peirce's account of abduction, the human mind is a biological system that provides it with a limited array of "admissible hypotheses" that are the foundations of human scientific inquiry—and by the same reasoning, of cognitive attainments generally. As a matter of simple logic, the system must exclude other hypotheses and ideas as inaccessible to us altogether, or too remote in some accessibility hierarchy to be accessible in fact, though they might be so for a differently structured mind—perhaps not Peirce's view. UG plays something of the same role for language, and the basic observation carries over for all biological capacities.

Peirce's concept of abduction is sometimes glossed as inference to the best explanation, but though undeveloped, the concept goes well beyond that. Crucially, Peirce insisted on *limits* of "admissible hypotheses," which he took to be quite narrow, a prerequisite for "imagining correct theories." He was concerned with growth of scientific knowledge, but the same holds for acquisition of commonsense understanding, of language acquisition in particular.[3]

The same should be expected to be true even of the questions that we can formulate; innate structure provides a rich variety of formulable questions, while barring others that some different mind might recognize to be the right ones to ask. I also cited the somewhat similar ideas of Hume, who recognized that just as for "beasts," so "the greater part of human knowledge" depends on "a species of natural instincts," which "derive from the original hand of nature"—in our terms, genetic endowment. The same conclusions follow.

All of this does seem to me close to truism, if perhaps not for reasons that have led many distinguished figures to somewhat similar conclusions. If we are biological organisms, not angels, then our cognitive faculties are similar to those called "physical capacities" and should be studied much as other systems of the body are.

Take, for example, the digestive system. Vertebrates have "a second brain," the "gut brain," the enteric nervous system, "an independent site of neural integration and processing." Its structure and component cells are "more akin to those of the brain than to those of any other peripheral organ." There are more nerve cells in the bowel than in the spine, in fact more "than in the entire remainder of our peripheral nervous system," 100 million in the small intestine alone. The gut brain is also a "vast chemical warehouse within which is represented every one of the classes of neurotransmitter found in the brain," with internal communication that is "rich and brainlike in its complexity." The gut is "the only organ that contains an intrinsic nervous system that is able to mediate reflexes in the complete absence of input from the brain or spinal cord." "The brain in the bowel has evolved in pace with the brain in the head." It has become "a vibrant, modern data-processing center that enables us to accomplish some very important and unpleasant tasks with no mental effort," and when we are lucky, to do so "efficiently and outside our consciousness." It is possible that it "may also have its own psychoneuroses," and some researchers today report that it is susceptible to such diseases of the brain as Alzheimer's, Parkinson's, and autism. It has its own sensory transducers and regulatory apparatus, which equip it to deal with specific tasks imposed by the organs with which it interacts, excluding others.[4]

Uncontroversially, "the original hand of nature" determines what the gut brain can and cannot do—the "problems" it can solve and the "mysteries" that are beyond its reach. Uncontroversially, scope and limits are related: the structural properties that provide scope also set limits. In the case of the gut brain, there are no debates about some obscure "innateness hypothesis"—which is often condemned in the case of language but never defended, because there is no such hypothesis apart from various ideas about what the genetic component is. There are no complaints that after all these years the genetic component of the gut brain is not fully understood—just as in other domains. The study of the gut brain is internalist. There is no philosophical critique based on the fact that what goes on in the digestive system crucially depends on matters external to it, elsewhere in the organism or outside the skin. One studies the nature of the internal system, and its external interactions, with no philosophical quandaries.

Comparable concerns are considered to pose serious dilemmas for the study of the first brain and its capacities, human language specifically. This seems to me one instance of a curious tendency to treat mental aspects of the human organism differently from so-called physical aspects, a kind of methodological dualism, which is more pernicious than Cartesian metaphysical dualism. The latter was a respectable scientific hypothesis, proven wrong when Newton undermined the mechanical philosophy of early modern science by demonstrating that one of the Cartesian substances—body—does not exist, thereby eliminating the mind-body problem, at least in its Cartesian form, and leaving open the question what the "physical" or "material" is supposed to be.[5] Methodological dualism in contrast seems to have nothing to recommend it. If we abandon it, then it is hard to see why the first brain, in particular its cognitive aspects, should be studied in some way that is fundamentally different from how one investigates the gut brain, or any other component of the body. If so, then mysterianism is just a variety of truism, along with internalism—contrary to views widely held.

For different and varying reasons, many distinguished figures have been guilty of accepting the truism of mysterianism. I suppose that one should include Bertrand Russell, ninety years ago, when he adopted the Humean view that "the highest grade [of certainty] belongs to my own percepts," and we can then think of the constructions of the mind as efforts to make sense of what we perceive, whether the reflexive constructions of commonsense understanding or the more considered and disciplined efforts of the sciences—which show us that what is "given" in perception is a construct from external data and mental structure, matters discussed interestingly by C. I. Lewis shortly after.[6]

As Hume put the matter, we must keep to the "Newtonian philosophy," with a "modest skepticism to a certain degree, and a fair confession of ignorance in subjects, that exceed all human capacity"—which for Hume includes virtually everything beyond appearances. We must "refrain from disquisitions concerning their real nature and operations." It is the imagination, "a kind of magical faculty in the soul, which . . . is inexplicable by the utmost efforts of human understanding," that leads us to believe that we experience external continuing objects, including a mind or self.[7] Contrary to Dr. Johnson, G. E. Moore, and other estimable figures, his reasoning seems to me to merit respect.

In a careful and informative study of Hume's appendix to the *Treatise*, Galen Strawson argues, convincingly I think, that Hume finally came to realize that the difficulties he faces are far deeper. "It is evident," Hume concluded, "that there is a principle of connection between the different thoughts or ideas in the mind," a real connection, not one feigned by the imagination. But there is no place for such a really existing entity in his philosophy/psychology, so at the end his "hopes vanished." His fundamental principles collapsed, irretrievably. One of the more poignant moments in the history of philosophy.[8]

For Russell, it followed that physics can only hope to discover "the causal skeleton of the world, [while studying] percepts only in their cognitive aspect; their other aspects lie outside its purview"—though we recognize their existence, at the highest grade of certainty in fact, whether or not we can find satisfactory explanations in our scientific endeavors.

All of this seems to be thoroughgoing mysterianism, perhaps modifying it by taking consciousness to be at the highest grade of certainty while everything else falls under problems, in part perhaps even mysteries-for-humans. That would include the quandaries regarded as the "hard problems" in the early days of modern science and philosophy, in the seventeenth and eighteenth centuries. The most troublesome of the hard problems in that era had to do with the nature of motion, of attraction and repulsion. The "hard problems" were never solved. Rather, they were abandoned, and regarded by the more perceptive observers, like Locke and Hume, as permanent mysteries—at least mysteries-for-humans, we might add.

That was well understood at the time. Locke wrote that while we remain in "incurable ignorance of what we desire to know" about matter and its effects, and no "science of bodies [that provides true explanations is] within our reach," he was "convinced by the judicious Mr. Newton's incomparable book, that it is too bold a presumption to limit God's power, in this point, by my narrow conceptions." Though gravitation of matter to matter is "inconceivable to me," nevertheless, as Newton demonstrated, we must recognize that it is within God's power "to put into bodies, powers and ways of operations, above what can be derived from our idea of body, or can be explained by what we know of matter." And thanks to Newton's work, we know that "he has done so."[9]

Given mysterian truisms, what is inconceivable to me is no criterion for what can exist. Dropping the theology, we can reformulate Locke's thoughts as holding that the natural world has properties that are mysteries-for-humans.

Newton did not disagree. In his constant search for some way to avoid the "absurd" conclusion that objects interact at a distance, he speculated that God, who is everywhere, might be the "immaterial agent" underlying gravitational interactions. But he could go no further, since he refused to "feign hypotheses" beyond what can be experimentally established. Newton agreed with his most eminent critic Leibniz that interaction without contact is "inconceivable," though he did not agree that it was an "unreasonable occult property," in Leibniz's words.[10] Newton held that his principles were not occult: "their causes only are occult." These causes might, he hoped, be accounted for in physical terms, meaning the terms of the mechanical philosophy or something like them. In the absence of that achievement, to derive general principles inductively from phenomena, Newton argued, and "to tell us how the properties of actions of all corporeal things follow from those manifest principles, would be a very great step in philosophy, though the causes of these principles were not yet discovered."

In his penetrating study of Newton as a philosopher, Andrew Janiak argues that Newton had independent reasons for rejecting interaction without contact. Newton's "understanding of God's place within the physical world," Janiak observes, "forms a metaphysical framework for his thinking in precisely the sense that it is not subject to revision through reflection on experience or through the development of physical science." And "if divine distant action is possible," yielding action at a distance, "then God's omnipotence need not be construed as Newton always construes it, in terms of divine omnipresence."

Later Newtonians rejected the metaphysics, hence accepting action at a distance within theoretical constructions while disregarding the "inconceivability" of the conclusions about the world that troubled Newton's great contemporaries, and also Newton himself.

Accordingly, the goals of scientific inquiry were implicitly restricted: from the kind of conceivability that was a criterion for true understanding in early modern science to something much narrower: intelligibility of theories about the world. This seems to me a step of considerable significance in the history of human thought and inquiry, more so than is generally recognized. It bears directly on the scope of mysterianism in the broad sense.

Locke went on to conclude that just as God added to matter such inconceivable properties as gravitational attraction, he might also have "superadded" to matter the capacity of thought. Replacing "God" by "nature" opens the topic to inquiry, a path that was pursued extensively in the years that followed, leading to the conclusion that thought is a property of certain forms of organized matter.[11] As Darwin restated the fairly common understanding, there is no need to regard thought, "a secretion of the brain," as "more wonderful than gravity, a property of matter"[12]—inconceivable to us, but that is a fact not about the external world but about our cognitive limitations.

Some of the early modern understanding of these matters has been rediscovered in recent years, sometimes with a sense of wonderment, as when Frances Crick formulated his "astonishing hypothesis" that our mental and emotional states are "in fact no more than the behavior of a vast assembly of nerve cells and their associated molecules." In the philosophical literature, this rediscovery has sometimes been regarded as a radical new idea in the study of mind. As Paul Churchland puts it, citing John Searle, the new idea is "the bold assertion that mental phenomena are entirely natural and caused by the neurophysiological activities of the brain." These proposals reiterate, in virtually the same words, formulations of centuries ago, after the traditional mind-body problem became unformulable with Newton's demolition of the only coherent notion of body (or physical, material, etc.): for example, Joseph Priestley's conclusion that properties "termed mental" reduce to "the organical structure of the brain," stated in different words by Locke, Darwin, and many others, and almost inescapable, it would seem, after the collapse of the mechanical philosophy that provided the foundations for early modern science.[13]

The last decade of the twentieth century was designated "the Decade of the Brain." In introducing a collection of essays reviewing its results, neuroscientist Vernon Mountcastle formulated the guiding theme as the thesis of the new biology that "things mental, indeed minds, are emergent properties of brains, [though] these emergences are . . . produced by principles that . . . we do not yet understand"—again reiterating eighteenth-century insights in virtually the same words.[14]

The phrase "we do not *yet* understand," however, should strike a note of caution. We might recall Bertrand Russell's observation in 1927 that chemical laws "cannot at present be reduced to physical laws," a fact that led eminent scientists to regard chemistry as no more than a mode of computation that could predict experimental results but not real science. As soon discovered, Russell's observation, though correct, was understated. Chemical laws were not in fact reducible to physical laws as physics was then understood, though after physics underwent radical changes, with the quantum-theoretic revolution, it was unified with a virtually unchanged chemistry.

There may well be lessons here for neuroscience and philosophy of mind. Contemporary neuroscience is hardly as well established as physics was a century ago. In fact, there are what seem to me to be cogent critiques of its foundational assumptions.[15] The common slogan that study of mind is *neuroscience* at an abstract level might turn out to be just as misleading as comparable statements about chemistry ninety years ago—if, that is, we have in mind today's neuroscience.

Note that questions that arise concerning this matter have no bearing on taking the mind to be the brain viewed at a certain level of abstraction, as in the discussion here.

Thomas Nagel, in recent work that has been highly controversial, writes that "mind, I suspect, is not an inexplicable accident or a divine and anomalous gift but a basic aspect of nature that we will not understand until we transcend the built-in limits of contemporary scientific orthodoxy."[16] If that turns out to be true, it would not be much of a departure from the history of science, though his invocation of "incredulity" and "common sense" should, I think, go the way of similar concerns that were abandoned from the late seventeenth century, as the import of Newton's discoveries was assimilated and the goals of scientific inquiry implicitly and significantly restricted, as discussed earlier.

In the light of these discoveries, and their implications, Hume wrote that Newton's greatest achievement was "to draw the veil from some of the mysteries of nature," while also having "restored [Nature's] ultimate secrets to that obscurity, in which they ever did and ever will remain."[17] For humans at least. All a form of dedicated mysterianism, for substantial reasons.

As for consciousness, it entered modern philosophical discourse at about the same time. In his recent comprehensive scholarly study of this range of topics, Udo Thiel finds that the first English philosopher to make extensive use of the noun "consciousness," with a philosophical meaning, was Ralph Cudworth, in the 1670s, though it was not until fifty years later that consciousness became an object of inquiry in its own right.[18] Subsequently consciousness was identified with thought, as it already had been by Descartes. And for some, like von Humboldt, thought was further identified with language, which provides the language of thought, ideas that can partially be reconstructed in contemporary terms, as I discussed in chapter 1.

In the modern period, identification of thought with consciousness reappears in various way, for example, in Quine's thesis that rule-following reduces either to "fitting," as the planets fit Kepler's laws, or to "guiding" by conscious thought. Or in Searle's "connection principle," holding that operations of the mind must be somehow accessible to conscious experience, an idea that is not easy to formulate coherently. Whether taken to be empirical claims or terminological stipulations, these doctrines rule out much of what has been discovered about rule-following in language or perception, for example, the rule of structure-dependence for language that I discussed in chapter 1, and, more important, its basis, or what Donald Hoffman in his study of visual intelligence calls "the rigidity rule," the rule that image projections are interpreted "as projections of rigid motions in three dimensions," even with highly impoverished stimuli.[19]

There is reason to believe that what reaches consciousness, even potentially, may well be just a scattered reflection of inaccessible mental processes, which interact intimately with the fragments that do sometimes reach consciousness. The now famous Libet experiments on decision making provide some independent evidence about this matter—though it is a mistake, I think, to regard them as having some bearing on freedom of will. The same issues largely remain, including considerations of personal responsibility, if decisions are made without conscious awareness or deliberation, including issues of possible cognitive limitations, to which I will return.

If it is true that fragments of mental processes that reach consciousness interact intimately with those that are inaccessible, as seems fairly clearly to be the case at least for use of language, then restriction of focus to conscious awareness, or accessibility to consciousness, may severely impede the development of a science of mind. These are topics of considerable interest, but there is no time to pursue them here.

Instead, let us return to mysterianism in the broad sense, not restricted to consciousness, taking it to be truism, as I think we should. We can consider various kinds of mysteries. Some are quite far-reaching, such as those I mentioned: perhaps permanent mysteries-for-humans. But before returning to these, it is worth considering others that are narrower: cases that might fall within our cognitive capacities and where there might in principle be relevant empirical evidence, though we cannot obtain it. Or cases where ethical considerations bar experiments that might answer questions we can sensibly pose. Thus a lot is known about the neurology of the human visual system thanks to invasive experiments on cats and monkeys, but we cannot learn about language this way. There is nothing homologous known in the animal world and relevant human experiments are barred, though perhaps some barriers might erode with new technology.

One example might be evolution of cognition—in particular, what is called "evolution of language," meaning evolution of the capacity for language, the language faculty; languages change but do not evolve. Evolutionary biologist Richard Lewontin argued extensively years ago that we will learn virtually nothing about these matters: "It might be interesting to know how cognition (whatever that is) arose and spread and changed," he concluded, "but we cannot know. Tough luck."[20] Relevant evidence isn't available to us. The editors of the MIT *Invitation to Cognitive Science* in which he published these conclusions found them persuasive, as I do, though his analysis, largely ignored, has not impeded the growth of a huge literature of what Lewontin calls "storytelling," particularly in the case of language.

The storytelling typically proceeds without even spelling out the essential nature of the phenotype, a prerequisite to any serious evolutionary inquiry. And it also typically constructs stories about communication, a different though perhaps more appealing topic, because one can at least imagine continuities and small changes in accord with conceptions of evolution that are conventional though dubious at best. A recent technical paper reviews what has been done since Lewontin's strictures, pretty much reaffirming them—plausibly I think, but then I am one of the authors.[21]

With regard to language origins, we know of one fact with considerable confidence and have another plausible surmise. The fact is that there has been no detectable evolution since our ancestors left Africa, perhaps 50,000 to 80,000 years ago. The same appears to be true of cognitive capacity more generally. The plausible surmise is Tattersall's, which I quoted in chapter 1: roughly 50,000 to 100,000 years before that, there is little reason to suppose that language existed at all.

An account of the origin of human language will have to respect the fact and at least attend to the surmise. It will have to provide some credible proposal as to the origin of what I called the Basic Property. There is none, to my knowledge, apart from what I mentioned in chapter 1, generally regarded as heretical, or worse.

There are also further tasks. One is to account for the variety of languages, for the range of options permitted by the evolved language faculty. Particularly in the past thirty years, that has become a rich and illuminating study of permissible parameters of variation—which themselves pose evolutionary problems.

A still more challenging problem is to account for the origins of the atoms of computation for the Basic Property. Here too there is extensive literature, but of questionable value, since it also rarely attends to the phenotype, the nature of meaning in human language. Investigation I think undermines some conventional doctrines and raises serious questions about evolution and acquisition.

The atoms of computation—call them "atomic concepts"—are word-like objects but not words. Words are constructed by the ancillary process of externalization, which does not feed the systems of thought, if the account I discussed in chapter 1 is correct. The atoms are sometimes called "lexical items," but that is not quite right either. The atoms of the syntactic computations that reach the conceptual-intentional interface do not have phonological properties, as lexical items do. These are assigned as an early step of externalization and are arbitrary, in the familiar Saussurean sense. Furthermore, as is now known, sound is only one possible modality for externalization.

More significantly, the "atomic concepts" for human language and thought seem to be quite different from anything found in systems of animal communication. The latter, it appears, are linked directly to entities that are extramental and can be identified independently of any consideration of the symbolic system itself. A vervet monkey, for example, has a number of calls. One is associated with fluttering of leaves, taken as a sign that a predator may be coming. Another might be associated with some hormonal change: "I'm hungry." This appears to be general and is quite different from human language, where even the simplest elements lack this property, contrary to a conventional *referentialist* doctrine holding that there is a direct relation between words and extramental entities, as illustrated in the titles of such standard works as Quine's *Word and Object* and Roger Brown's *Words and Things*, and an extensive literature.

Returning to Cartesian reflections on mind, animal signaling appears to be *caused* by circumstances, internal and external, while for humans, appropriate production of words and more complex expressions is at most *incited or inclined.*

Furthermore, the associations for animal symbol systems are of a kind quite different from anything in human language. In this respect, Darwin's characterization of the uniqueness of human language, which I quoted in chapter 1, has to be modified beyond what he could have anticipated. One of the leading specialists on the topic, Laura-Ann Petitto, who was the primary investigator in the NIM project, writes that

> chimps, unlike humans, use such labels in a way that seems to rely heavily on some global notion of association. A chimp will use the same label *apple* to refer to the action of eating apples, the location where apples are kept, events and locations of objects other than apples that happened to be stored with an apple (the knife used to cut it), and so on and so forth—all simultaneously, and without apparent recognition of the relevant differences or the advantages of being able to distinguish among them. Even the first words of the young human baby are used in a kind-

concept constrained way.... But the usage of chimps, even after years of training and communication with humans, never displays this sensitivity to differences among natural kinds. Surprisingly, then, chimps do not really have "names for things" at all. They have only a hodge-podge of loose associations.[22]

Human language is radically different, except in one respect: it also doesn't have names for things, though for different reasons. The atomic concepts of human language do not pick out entities of the extramental world. There is apparently no notion "reference" or "denotation" for human language, though there are of course actions of referring and denoting—an observation that has not been ignored in the philosophical literature: Peter Strawson's paper on reference and referring sixty years ago is one well-known example, or Julius Moravcsik's *aitiational* semantics twenty years later, or Akeel Bilgrami's discussion of the "radically local or contextual" notion of content twenty years after that.[23] One can posit a circumstance-dependent relation of reference deriving from acts of referring; thus the name "Jones" refers to the person Jones (far from an innocent notion, of course) insofar as we refer to him by using the name in some way in some particular circumstances. But the act of referring is the fundamental notion.

In this respect, atomic concepts are rather like the elements of phonetic representation. We can think of these as instructions to articulators (and comparably, the perceptual apparatus). The act of pronunciation yields a specific event in the mind-independent world, but it would be idle to seek some mind-independent entity or category to which the phonetic unit corresponds even for a single individual, let alone a community of users. Acoustic and articulatory phonetics seek to discover how internal symbols enter into the production and interpretation of sounds, no simple task; after sixty years of intensive study with high-tech instrumentation, a great deal remains unknown. There is no reason to suspect that it would be an easier task to discover how internal systems are used to talk or think about aspects of the world. Quite the contrary, as becomes clear when we actually investigate the atomic concepts of linguistic and cognitive computation, and the ways they are used to refer.

That much was already clear to Aristotle. He concluded that we can "define a house as stones, bricks and timbers," in terms of material constitution, but also as "a receptacle to shelter chattels and living beings," in terms of function and design; and we should combine both parts of the definition, integrating matter and form, since the "essence of a house" involves the "purpose and end" of the material constitution.[24] Hence a house is not a mind-independent object. That becomes still clearer when we investigate further and discover that the concept *house* has much more intricate properties, an observation that generalizes far beyond. Inquiry reveals that even the simplest expressions have quite intricate meanings.[25]

In other domains, the referentialist doctrine does have a valuable role. In metamathematics, for example. And in the sciences, where the doctrine is taken to be a guiding norm. In devising technical notions like *electron* and *phoneme*, researchers hope to be identifying entities that exist in the world. But none of this should be confused with human language. Further confusions can arise if these different systems are intermingled. Thus chemists freely use the term "water" in informal discourse but not in the sense of the word of natural language, which also violates the referentialist doctrine.

Note that Aristotle was defining the entity *house*, not the word "house." For him, it was a matter of metaphysics: the entity is a combination of matter and form. In the course of the cognitive revolution of the seventeenth century, the general point of view shifted toward seeking the "innate cognoscitive powers" that enter into our understanding of experience. Summarizing many years of discussion of such topics, Hume concluded that "the identity we ascribe" to minds, vegetables, animal bodies, and other entities is "only a fictitious one" established by the imagination "upon like objects," not a "peculiar nature belonging to this form."[26]

One illustration of the deficiencies of the referentialist doctrine is the concept *person*, intensively studied since the classical era, particularly since the seventeenth century. Thus when one says that the name "Jones" denotes its bearer, what exactly is the bearer? It cannot simply be the material body. As Locke observes, there is no absurdity in thinking that the same person might have two different bodies: if the same consciousness "can be transferred from one thinking substance to another, it will be possible that two thinking substances may make up one person." And there are many other complications. Personal identity thus consists (at least) in some kind of "identity of consciousness," in psychic continuity. Locke adds that the term "person" (or "self" or "soul") is, furthermore, "a forensic term, appropriating actions and their merit; and so belongs only to intelligent agents, capable of a law, and happiness, and misery."[27]

There is no time here to discuss the rich and perceptive inquiries on the topic, reviewed recently in the work by Udo Thiel that I mentioned earlier. It may however be useful to add a few reminders on the interesting legal history of personhood as a "forensic" concept.

The Fifth Amendment to the American Constitution guarantees the rights of "persons": crucially, that they shall not be "deprived of life, liberty, or property, without due process of law," provisions that trace back to Magna Carta. But the concept *person* was sharply circumscribed. It plainly did not include Native Americans or slaves. Or women. Under British common law, taken over by the colonies, women were basically property: of their father, handed over to their husbands. The prevailing concept was expressed by Kant a few years later: women have no "civil personality" because they depend for their living "on the offices of others," like apprentices and servants, who also lack "civil personality."

The Fourteenth Amendment extended personhood to freed slaves, at least in principle. In reality, a few years later a North–South compact permitted the slaveholding states to reinstitute a form of slavery by effectively criminalizing black life, providing a cheap and disciplined labor force for much of the industrial revolution, a system that persisted until World War II created the need for free labor. The ugly history is being reenacted under the vicious "drug war" of the past generation, since Ronald Reagan.

As for women, it was not until 1975 that the Supreme Court recognized women to be "peers," with the guaranteed right to serve on federal juries—hence advancing to the category of full personhood. Recent court decisions extend the right of personhood that had already granted to corporations, while excluding undocumented aliens from the category.[28] It would be no great surprise if chimpanzees are granted the rights of persons before undocumented immigrants are.

In brief, understanding "person" to be a forensic term has many complex and troublesome human consequences.

Returning to language and atomic concepts, recent studies of acquisition, particularly by Lila Gleitman and her associates, have shown that meanings of even the most elementary linguistic expressions are acquired from very restricted evidence, and very rapidly during the early years of life, even under severe sensory constraints. It is difficult to see how one can avoid the conclusion that these intricate structures depend on "innate cognoscitive powers" of the kinds explored in interesting ways in the "first cognitive revolution" of the seventeenth century. Intricacies mount rapidly when we proceed beyond the simple elements used to refer, reinforcing the conclusion that innate properties of the mind play a critical role in their acquisition and use. Such considerations seem impossible to reconcile with familiar views of language acquisition as based on ostension, instruction, and habit formation; or with what Dagfinn Føllesdal, in his penetrating study of Quine's theory of meaning, calls the "MMM thesis: *The meaning of a linguistic expression is the joint product of all the evidence that helps learners and users of the language determine that meaning.*"[29] In an appreciative comment, Quine endorses Føllesdal's interpretation but with a crucial modification, stating that "what matters is just that linguistic meaning is a function of observable behavior in observable circumstances." The qualification, however, leaves a very weak thesis, one that would be true no matter how rich the crucial innate endowment and how impoverished the data, as long at least some stimuli are necessary, just as the mature visual system is a function of visual input.

If conclusions of the kind just mentioned do indeed generalize, as appears to be the case, then it would follow that natural language has no referential semantics in the sense of relations between symbols and mind-independent entities. Rather, it has syntax (internal symbol manipulation) and pragmatics (modes of use of language). Formal semantics, including model-theoretic semantics, falls under syntax in this categorization. It is motivated by external world considerations, just as phonology is, but relates to the world only in the context of theories of action, so it appears.

Considerations of this nature pose very serious problems for any potential theory of the origin of language. As I mentioned, it appears to be the case that animal communication systems are based on a one-to-one relation between mind/brain processes and "an aspect of the environment to which these processes adapt the animal's behavior."[30] If so, the gap between human language and animal communication is as dramatic in this domain as in the domains of language structure, acquisition, and use, and inquiry into origins will have to look elsewhere.

Let's turn briefly to the objects to which a speaker refers. We have to ask what qualifies. Quine was concerned with this topic. He observed that in some cases a noun phrase may not be "a compelling candidate—on the surface, anyway—for thinghood," as Daniel Dennett put the matter recently in discussing the issues Quine raised. We say "for Pete's sake" or "for the sake of" but don't expect to answer thing-related questions about sakes or about Pete, for example, "how many sakes are there?" or "how tall is Pete?" Similarly, Dennett observes, "Paris and London plainly exist, but do the *miles* that separate them also exist?" Quine's answer, Dennett writes, is that a noun phrase of this kind is "*defective*, and its putative reference need not be taken seriously from an ontological point of view."[31]

Often there is direct linguistic evidence of deficiency of "thinghood." Consider the nouns "flaw" and "fly." In some constructions, they function in similar ways: *there is a fly in the bottle / a flaw in the argument*; *there is believed to be a fly in the bottle / a flaw in the argument.* In others not: *there is a fly believed to be in the bottle / *a flaw believed to be in the argument*; *a fly is in the bottle / *a flaw is in the argument* (* indicating deviance). Some constructions carry a kind of existential import that is lacking in others, even those with explicit existential expressions, a matter that falls within an explanatory framework with a variety of consequences, discussed elsewhere.[32]

There do seem to be distinctions among "candidates for thinghood," but questions soon arise. Presumably at least the word "thing" should be a compelling candidate for thinghood. But what are the identity conditions for things, and how many are there? Suppose we see some branches strewn on the ground. If they fell from a tree after a storm, they are not a thing. But if they were carefully placed there by an artist as a work of conceptual art, perhaps given a name, then the construction is a thing (and might win an award). A little thought will show that many complex factors determine whether some part of the world constitutes a thing, including human intention and design—Aristotelian *form*—which are not properties that can be detected by study of the mind-independent world. If *thing* does not qualify for *thinghood* independently of mind-dependent circumstances, then what does?

What about Dennett's examples Paris and London? We can refer to them, as if I were to say that that I visited London the year before it was destroyed by a great fire and then rebuilt with entirely different materials and design fifty miles up the Thames, where I intend to revisit it next year. Evidently, the extramental world does not contain an entity with such properties, an entity that a physicist could in principle discover. We can however refer to London, either by using the expression "London" or a pronoun linked to it, or by employing some more complex phrase, say, "my favorite city." In my I-language, there is an internal entity *London*—not necessarily matching yours exactly—constituted of elements that provide perspectives for referring to aspects of the world, much as the features of the internal phonetic entity [ta] provide means for me to pronounce and interpret certain events in the world. In these terms, many classical paradoxes become difficult or impossible to formulate, from Plutarch's Ship of Theseus to Kripke's puzzles, all stated in terms of referentialist assumptions.

As Norbert Hornstein suggests, we might reframe the observation, taking the problematic features of the paradoxes to be another argument against the referentialist assumptions that lead to them.

Early investigation of these topics was concerned primarily with individuation: What makes an individual distinct from others? With the rise of corpuscular theories in the seventeenth century, the focus of investigation shifted from individuation to the prior question of identity: What makes an individual the same through time despite partial changes? For a corpuscularian, an individual just is what it is—a "distinct portion of matter which a number of (corpuscles) ... make up" (Robert Boyle). Study of identity through time led to a cognitive treatment of the issue. As Thiel puts it, "as substantial forms are denied and no 'principle' of identity could be discovered in the things themselves, it is recognized that their identity must depend on what we regard as their essential constituents"—"on what we regard," that is, on our criteria for judging, on our concepts of things. This "subjectivist revolution" was carried forward particularly by Locke, for whom existence is preserved "under the same denomination," in terms of the abstract ideas under which we consider the world.

Hume interprets our tendency to assign identity through time as a "natural propension," a kind of instinct, which constructs experience to conform to our modes of cognition—and in ways that seem sharply different from anything in the animal world. The "propension" to ascribe identity where evidence shows diversity "is so great," Hume writes, that imagination creates concepts that bind a succession of related objects together, leading us "to imagine something unknown and mysterious, connecting the parts." Hence ascription of identity is a construction of the imagination, and the factors that enter into constructing these fictions become a topic of cognitive science, though Hume might have demurred if the imagination is indeed, as he thought, "a kind of magical faculty... [that]... is inexplicable by the utmost efforts of human understanding,"[33] hence yet another mystery-for-humans.

In these terms, it should also be possible to reinterpret the rich and illuminating record of thinking about the nature of the soul, though now divorced of the theological conditions, like resurrection, and from the metaphysical framework of earlier years.

These are all matters that seem to me to deserve considerably more attention and concern than they have received. In particular, they pose very serious problems for the study of acquisition and origin of language, perhaps unsolvable ones in the latter case, for Lewontin's reasons.

These early modern reflections on the origins of knowledge led to a much more fundamental form of mysterianism, the kind I have been sampling briefly. For Locke and Hume, it follows from epistemological considerations that the limits of our understanding are very narrow. Janiak observes that Newton regarded such global skepticism as "irrelevant—he takes the possibility of our knowledge of nature for granted." Hence "the primary epistemic questions confronting us are raised by physical theory itself." That would exclude the skeptical stance of Locke and Hume. They, however, took quite seriously the new science-based mysterianism that arose from Newton's demolition of the mechanical philosophy, which had provided the very criterion of intelligibility for the scientific revolution of the seventeenth century, based on the conception of the world as an elaborate machine. Galileo insisted that theories are intelligible only under a very restrictive condition: only if we can "duplicate [their posits] by means of appropriate artificial devices," a conception that was maintained by Descartes, Leibniz, Huygens, Newton, and other great figures of the scientific revolution.

Accordingly, Newton's discoveries left the world unintelligible when his theological assumptions were dismissed. The solution reached, as mentioned earlier, was to lower the goals of science, abandoning the search for intelligibility of the world in favor of something much weaker: theories that are intelligible to us whether or not what they posit is intelligible. It was then quite natural for Bertrand Russell to dismiss the very idea of an intelligible world as "absurd," no longer a reasonable goal for scientific inquiry.

There is no contradiction in supposing that we might be able to probe the limits of human understanding and try to sharpen the boundary between problems and mysteries (for humans).[34] Experimental inquiry might be able to determine the "limits on admissible hypotheses" that Peirce discussed, both those that enter into commonsense understanding and those that constitute what might be called our "science-forming capacity," Peirce's specific interest, which might well have different properties (a matter that is contested in cognitive psychology).[35] One approach would be to take seriously the concerns of the great figures of the early scientific revolution and the Enlightenment: what they found "inconceivable," and particularly their reasons. The "mechanical philosophy" itself has a claim to be an approximation to commonsense understanding of the world. Despite much sophisticated commentary, it is also hard to escape the force of Descartes's conviction that free will is "the noblest thing" we have, that "there is nothing we comprehend more evidently and more perfectly," and that "it would be absurd" to doubt something that "we comprehend intimately, and experience within ourselves" merely because it is "by its nature incomprehensible to us," if indeed we do not "have intelligence enough" to understand the workings of mind, as he speculated.[36] Concepts of determinacy and randomness fall within our intellectual grasp, but if "free actions of men" that are "undetermined" cannot be accommodated in these terms, that could turn out to be a matter of cognitive limitations—which would not preclude an intelligible theory of such actions, far as this is from today's scientific understanding.

While the list of mysterians is long and distinguished, their stance appears to contrast with the exuberant thesis that the early scientific revolution and the Enlightenment provided humans with limitless explanatory power, exhibited in the rapid development of modern science. One outstanding figure who espoused this view was David Hilbert. In his final lecture in 1930, not long before the Nazi plague destroyed the Hilbert Circle in Göttingen, he recalled "the magnificent manner of thinking and of the world-view that shines forth" in the words of the great mathematician Carl Gustav Jacob Jacobi, who admonished Joseph Fourier for holding that the goal of mathematics was to explain natural phenomena. Rather, Hilbert urged, "the sole aim of all science is the honor of the human spirit," and so "a problem of pure number theory is every bit as valuable as a problem with practical applications." Whoever grasps this manner of thinking, Hilbert continued, will realize that "there is no *ignorabimus*," either in mathematics or in natural science. "There are absolutely no unsolvable problems. Instead of the foolish *ignorabimus* our answer is on the contrary: We must know, We shall know"—words that were engraved on Hilbert's tombstone.[37]

The prediction did not fare too well in mathematics, as Kurt Gödel soon demonstrated to the shock of the mathematical world. And despite the nobility of the thought, the argument has little force for the natural sciences.

Recently, physicist David Deutsch wrote that potential progress is "unbounded," as a result of the great achievement of the Enlightenment and early modern science: directing inquiry to the quest for good explanations, along Popperian lines. As David Albert expounds his thesis, "with the introduction of that particular habit of concocting and evaluating new hypotheses, there was a sense in which we could do anything. The capacities of a community that has mastered that method to survive, and to learn, and to remake the world according to its inclinations, are (in the long run) literally, mathematically, infinite."[38]

The quest for better explanations may well indeed be infinite, but infinite is of course not the same as limitless. English is infinite but doesn't include Greek. The integers are an infinite set but do not include the reals. I cannot discern an argument that addresses the range of mysterian concerns and conclusions.

The basic assumptions trace back at least to Peirce, who did however offer an argument, one related to Albert's observation about mastering the method to survive. Peirce proposed that the abductive instinct that establishes admissible hypotheses and allows us to choose among them developed through natural selection: variants that yielded truths about the world provided a selectional advantage and were retained during descent with modification, while others fell away. That belief, however, is completely unsustainable. On the contrary, the theory of evolution places humans firmly within the natural world, taking humans to be biological organisms, much like others, hence with capacities that have scope and limits, including the cognitive domain. Those who accept modern biology should therefore be mysterians.[39]

Dropping the untenable recourse to natural selection, we are left with a serious and challenging scientific inquiry: to determine the innate components of our cognitive nature in language, perception, concept formation, theory construction, artistic creation, and all other domains of life. A further task is to determine the scope and limits of human understanding, while recognizing that some differently structured intelligence might regard human mysteries as simple problems and wonder that we cannot find the answers, much as we can observe the inability of rats to run prime number mazes because of the very design of their cognitive nature.

Far from bewailing the existence of mysteries-for-humans, we should be extremely grateful for it. With no limits to abduction, our cognitive capacities would also have no scope, just as if the genetic endowment imposed no constraints on growth and development of an organism, it could become only a shapeless amoeboid creature, reflecting accidents of an unanalyzed environment. The conditions that prevent a human embryo from becoming an insect play a critical role in determining that it can become a human, and the same holds in the cognitive domain. Classical aesthetic theory recognized the same relation between scope and limits. Without rules, there can be no genuinely creative activity, even when creative work challenges and revises prevailing rules.

Honesty should lead us to concede, I think, that we understand little more about creativity than the Spanish physician-philosopher Juan Huarte did in the sixteenth century, when he distinguished the kind of intelligence humans shared with animals from the higher grade that humans alone possess and is illustrated in the creative use of language, and proceeding beyond that, from the still higher grade illustrated in true artistic and scientific creativity.[40] Nor do we even know whether these are questions that fall within the scope of human understanding, or whether they are among what Hume took to be Nature's ultimate secrets, consigned to "that obscurity in which they ever did and ever will remain."

3 | WHAT IS THE COMMON GOOD?

IN CHAPTERS 1 AND 2, I looked at the closely related topics of language and thought. Close inquiry reveals, I think, that they have many striking properties, for the most part hidden from direct observation and in important respects not accessible to consciousness. Among these are the basic structure and design of the underlying computational system of the "language of thought" provided by the internal language, the I-language, that each person has mastered, with rich but bounded scope determined by our essential nature. Furthermore, the atoms of computation, the atomic concepts of language and thought, appear to be unique to humans in fundamental respects, raising difficult problems about their origins, problems that cannot be productively investigated unless the properties of the phenotype are carefully taken into account. Inquiry reveals as well, I think, that the reach of human thought is itself bounded by the "limits on admissible hypotheses" that yield its richness and depth, leaving mysteries that will resist the kind of understanding to which creators of the early modern scientific revolution aspired, as was recognized in various ways by the great figures of seventeenth- and eighteenth-century thought; and also opening possibilities for research into intriguing questions that have been too little explored.

I have so far been keeping to certain cognitive aspects of human nature, and thinking of people as individuals. But of course humans are social beings, and the kind of creatures we become depends crucially on the social, cultural, and institutional circumstances of our lives. We are therefore led to inquire into the social arrangements that are conducive to the rights and welfare of people, to fulfilling their just aspirations—in brief, the common good.

I have also been keeping largely to what seem to me virtual truisms, though of an odd kind, since they are generally rejected. I'd like to suggest some more of these here, with the same odd features. And with the broader scope of the concerns I will try to address, these alleged truisms relate to an interesting category of ethical principles: those that are not only universal, in that they are virtually always professed, but doubly universal, in that at the same time they are almost universally rejected in practice. These range from very general principles, such as the truism that we should apply to ourselves the same standards we do to others, if not harsher ones, to more specific doctrines, such as dedication to promoting justice and human rights, proclaimed almost universally, even by the worst monsters, though the actual record is grim, across the spectrum.

A good place to start is with Mill's classic *On Liberty*. Its epigraph formulates "the grand, leading principle, towards which every argument unfolded in these pages directly converges: the absolute and essential importance of human development in its richest diversity." The words are quoted from

Wilhelm von Humboldt, one of the founders of classical liberalism among many other accomplishments. It follows that institutions that constrain such human development are illegitimate, unless they can somehow justify themselves.

Humboldt was expressing views that were familiar during the Enlightenment. Another illustration is Adam Smith's sharp critique of division of labor, and particularly his reasons.[1] In his words, "The understandings of the greater part of men are necessarily formed by their ordinary employments," and that being so,

> the man whose life is spent in performing a few simple operations, of which the effects too are, perhaps, always the same, or very nearly the same, has no occasion to exert his understanding ... and generally becomes as stupid and ignorant as it is possible for a human creature to be.... But in every improved and civilized society this is the state into which the labouring poor, that is, the great body of the people, must necessarily fall, unless government takes some pains to prevent it.

Concern for the common good should impel us to find ways to overcome the devilish impact of these disastrous policies, from the educational system to the conditions of work, providing opportunities to exert the understanding and cultivate human development in its richest diversity.

Smith's sharp critique of division of labor is not as well known as his fulsome praise for its great benefits. In fact, in the University of Chicago Press's scholarly bicentennial edition, it isn't even listed in the index. But it is an instructive illustration of Enlightenment ideals that are founding principles of classical liberalism.

Smith perhaps felt that it should not be too difficult to institute such humane policies as these. He opens his *Moral Sentiments* by observing that "however selfish soever man may be supposed, there are evidently some principles in his nature, which interest him in the fortune of others, and render their happiness necessary to him, though he derives nothing from it, except the pleasure of seeing it." Despite the power of the "vile maxim of the masters of mankind"—"All for ourselves, and nothing for other people"—the more benign "original passions of human nature" might compensate for that pathology.[2]

Classical liberalism was wrecked on the shoals of capitalism, but its humanistic commitments and aspirations did not die. In the modern period, similar ideas are reiterated, for example, by an important political thinker who described what he called "a definite trend in the historic development of mankind," which strives for "the free unhindered unfolding of all the individual and social forces in life." The author was Rudolf Rocker, a leading twentieth-century anarchist thinker and activist.[3] He was outlining an anarchist tradition culminating in his view in anarcho-syndicalism—in European terms, a variety of "libertarian socialism." These ideas, he held, do not depict "a fixed, self-enclosed social system" with a definite answer to all the multifarious questions and problems of human life but rather a trend in human development that strives to attain Enlightenment ideals.

The terms of political discourse are hardly models of precision. Considering the way the terms are used, it is next to impossible to give meaningful answers to such questions as "what is socialism?" Or capitalism, or free markets, or others in common usage. That is even truer of the term "anarchism." It has been subject to widely varied use, and outright abuse both by bitter enemies and those who hold its banner high, so much so that it resists any straightforward characterization. But I think Rocker's formulation captures leading ideas that animate at least some major currents of the rich and complex and often contradictory traditions of anarchist thought and action.

So understood, anarchism is the inheritor of the classical liberal ideas that emerged from the Enlightenment. It is part of a broader range of libertarian socialist thought and action that ranges from the left anti-Bolshevik Marxism of Anton Pannekoek, Karl Korsch, Paul Mattick, and others, to the anarcho-syndicalism that crucially includes the practical achievements of revolutionary Spain in 1936, reaching further to worker-owned enterprises spreading today in the Rust Belt of the United States, in northern Mexico, in Egypt, and in many other countries, most extensively in the Basque country in Spain, also encompassing the many cooperative movements around the world and a good part of feminist and civil and human rights initiatives.

This broad tendency in human development seeks to identify structures of hierarchy, authority, and domination that constrain human development, and then to subject them to a very reasonable challenge: justify yourself. Demonstrate that you are legitimate, either in some special circumstances at a particular stage of society or in principle. And if they cannot meet that challenge, they should be dismantled. And not just dismantled but also reconstructed, and for anarchists, "refashioned from below," as Nathan Schneider observes in a recent commentary on anarchism.[4]

In part this sounds like truism: Why should anyone defend illegitimate structures and institutions? The perception is correct; the principle should be regarded as truism. But truisms at least have the merit of being true, which distinguishes them from a good deal of political discourse. And I think these truisms provide some useful stepping stones to finding the common good.

These particular truisms belong to the interesting category of moral principles that I mentioned earlier: those that are doubly universal. Among these is the truism that we should challenge coercive institutions and reject those that cannot demonstrate their legitimacy, dismantling them and reconstructing them from below. It is hard to see how it can plausibly be rejected in principle, though as usual to act on the principle is not as easy as to enunciate it grandly.

Proceeding with the same thoughts, again quoting Rocker, anarchism "seeks to free labor from economic exploitation" and to free society from "ecclesiastical or political guardianship," thereby opening the way to "an alliance of free groups of men and women based on cooperative labor and a planned administration of things in the interest of the community." As an anarchist *activist*, Rocker goes on to call on popular organizations to create "not only the ideas but also the facts of the future itself" within the present society, following Bakunin's injunction.

A traditional anarchist slogan is "Ni Dieu, ni Maître"—No God, no Master—a phrase that Daniel Guerin took as the title of his valuable collection of anarchist classics. I think it is fair to understand the slogan "No God" in Rocker's terms: opposition to ecclesiastical *guardianship*. Individual beliefs are a different matter. That leaves open the door to the lively and impressive tradition of Christian anarchism—for example, Dorothy Day's Catholic Workers Movement. And to many achievements of the liberation theology that was initiated half a century ago in Vatican II, igniting a vicious U.S. war against the church to destroy the heresy of a return to the radical pacifist message of the Gospels. The war was a success, according to the School of the Americas (since renamed), which trains Latin American killers and torturers and boasts triumphantly that the U.S. Army helped defeat liberation theology.[5] So it did, leaving a trail of religious martyrs, part of a hideous plague of repression that consumed the hemisphere.

Most of this is out of conventional history, because of the fallacy of wrong agency. We would know the details very well if the crimes could be attributed to an official enemy, another illustration of those interesting doubly universal ethical principles.

Genuine scholarship, of course, is well aware that from 1960 until "the Soviet collapse in 1990, the numbers of political prisoners, torture victims, and executions of nonviolent political dissenters in Latin America vastly exceeded those in the Soviet Union and its East European satellites. In other words, from 1960 to 1990, the Soviet Bloc as a whole was less repressive, measured in terms of human victims, than many individual Latin American countries, . . . an unprecedented human catastrophe" in Central America alone, particularly during the Reagan years.[6]

Among those executed were many religious martyrs, and there were mass slaughters as well, consistently supported or initiated by Washington. The reasons for the plague of repression had little to do with the Cold War, as we discover when we look beyond the standard rhetorical framework; rather, it was a reaction to the fact that subjects were daring to raise their heads, inspired in part by the return of the church to the "preferential option of the poor" of the Gospels.

Dostoyevsky's parable of the Grand Inquisitor comes at once to mind.

The phrase "No Master" is different: it refers not to individual belief, but to a social relation, a relation of subordination and dominance that anarchism seeks to dismantle and rebuild from below, unless it can somehow meet the harsh burden of establishing its legitimacy.

By now, we have departed from truism to ample controversy. In particular, at this point the American brand of libertarianism departs sharply from the libertarian tradition, accepting and indeed advocating the subordination of working people to the masters of the economy, and the subjection of everyone to the restrictive discipline and destructive features of markets. These are topics worth pursuing, but I will put them aside here, while noting that there may be ways to bring together the energies of libertarian left and right—as is sometimes done, for example in the valuable theoretical and practical work of economist David Ellerman.[7]

Anarchism is, famously, opposed to the state, while advocating "planned administration of things in the interest of the community," in Rocker's words; and beyond that, wide-ranging federations of self-governing communities and workplaces. In the real world of today, anarchists dedicated to these goals often support state power to protect people, society, and the earth itself from the ravages of concentrated private capital. Take, say, a venerable anarchist journal like *Freedom*, established as a journal of anarchist socialism by followers of Kropotkin in 1886. Opening its pages, we find that many are devoted to defending these rights, often by invoking state power, like regulation of safety and health and environmental protection.

There is no contradiction here. People live and suffer and endure in the real world of existing society, and any decent person should favor employing what means are available to safeguard and benefit them, even if a long-term goal is to displace these devices and construct preferable alternatives. In discussing such concerns, I have sometimes borrowed an image used by the Brazilian rural workers movement.[8] They speak of widening the floors of the cage, the cage of existing coercive institutions that can be widened by popular struggle, as has happened effectively over many years. And we can extend the image to think of the cage of coercive state institutions as a protection from savage beasts roaming outside, the predatory state-supported capitalist institutions that are dedicated in principle to the vile maxim of the masters, to private gain, power, and domination, with the interest of the community and its members at most a footnote, perhaps revered in rhetoric but dismissed in practice as a matter of principle and even law.

It is also worth remembering that the states that anarchists condemned were actually existing states, not visions of unrealized democratic dreams, such as government of, by, and for the people. They bitterly opposed the rule of what Bakunin called "the red bureaucracy," which he predicted, all too accurately, would be among the most savage of human creations. And they also opposed parliamentary systems that are instruments of class rule: the contemporary United States, for example. Some of the most respected work in academic political science compares attitudes and policy, the latter evident, the former accessible in careful polling that yields fairly consistent results. The most detailed current work reveals that the majority of the population is effectively disenfranchised.[9] About 70 percent, at the lower end of the wealth/income scale, have no influence on policy. As we move up the scale, influence slowly increases, and at the very top we reach those who pretty much determine policy, by means that are not obscure. The resulting system is not democracy but plutocracy.

Recognition of the fact is so deeply internalized that it becomes virtually invisible, sometimes in remarkable ways. Consider health care, which for years has ranked high among concerns of Americans. And for good reasons. The health-care system is a scandal. It has about twice the per capita costs of the health-care systems of OECD countries, along with relatively poor outcomes, and is a tremendous drain on the economy. It is also the only system that is largely privatized and unregulated.

The facts are noted in instructive ways. A review of the health-care fiasco in the *New York Times* observes that the United States "is fundamentally handicapped in its quest for cheaper health care: All other developed countries rely on a large degree of direct government intervention, negotiation or rate-setting to achieve lower-priced medical treatment for all citizens. That is not politically acceptable here." An expert is quoted as tracing the complexity of the Affordable Care Act to "the political need in the U.S. to rely on the private market to provide health care access." One consequence is "Kafkaesque" bills because "even Medicare is not allowed to negotiate drug prices for its tens of millions of beneficiaries."

The problem of "political impossibility" has been noted before. Thus in the 2004 presidential campaign, the *New York Times* reported, candidate John Kerry "took pains . . . to say that his plan for expanding access to health insurance would not create a new government program," because "there is so little political support for government intervention in the health care market in the United States."[10]

Why is government intervention, even negotiation to set drug prices, "not politically acceptable here"? Why does it have "so little political support"? As polls have made clear for years, that is not because of public opinion. Quite the contrary. Thus 85 percent of the public favor "allowing the federal government to negotiate with drug companies to try to get lower drug prices for seniors." When President Obama abandoned a public option, it had about 60 percent popular support. In past years, there has been very high public support for a national health plan of the kind familiar in developed countries, sometimes poorer ones as well. Support has been so high that in the late Reagan years, more than 70 percent of the public "thought health care should be a constitutional guarantee," while 40 percent "thought it already was."[11]

The tacit understanding is that "political support" means support by the pharmaceutical corporations and financial institutions. They determine what is "politically acceptable." In short, plutocracy, rising to the level of virtual necessary truth.

Or perhaps, a little more kindly, it is what British legal scholar Conor Gearty calls "neo-democracy," a partner of neoliberalism, a system in which liberty is enjoyed by the few and security in its fullest sense is available only to the elite, but within a system of more general formal rights.[12] It is a society that is free in the Hobbesian sense that a person "is not hindered to do what he has a will to do," and "if I choose not to do something merely because I dread the consequences, this does not mean that I am not free to do it; it merely means that I do not want to, that is, I am still free," so Hobbes explains. If the choice is starvation or servitude, and nothing hinders the choice, then we are free; it is merely that we do not choose starvation, dreading the consequences.

In contrast, a truly democratic system would seek to achieve the Humboldtian ideal. It might well have the character of "an alliance of free groups of men and women based on cooperative labor and a planned administration of things in the interest of the community," quoting Rocker again. In fact, that is not so remote from at least one version of the democratic ideal. One version. I will return to others.

Take, for example, John Dewey, whose major social and political concerns were democracy and education. No one took Dewey to be an anarchist. But consider his ideas.[13] In his conception of democracy, illegitimate structures of coercion must be dismantled. That includes, crucially, domination by "business for private profit through private control of banking, land, industry, reinforced by command of the press, press agents and other means of publicity and propaganda." He recognized that "power today resides in control of the means of production, exchange, publicity, transportation and communication. Whoever owns them rules the life of the country," even if democratic forms remain. Until those institutions are in the hands of the public, politics will remain "the shadow cast on society by big business," much as we see today.

But Dewey went well beyond calling for some form of public control. In a free and democratic society, he wrote, workers should be "the masters of their own industrial fate," not tools rented by employers, nor directed by state authorities. That position traces back to leading ideas of classical liberalism articulated by Humboldt and Smith, among others, and extended in the anarchist tradition.

Turning to education, Dewey held that it is "illiberal and immoral" to train children to work "not freely and intelligently, but for the sake of the work earned"—to achieve test scores for example—in which case their activity is "not free because not freely participated in." To use imagery dating from the Enlightenment, education should not be a matter of pouring water into a vessel—and a very leaky vessel as we have all experienced—but rather, to borrow from von Humboldt again, it should be conceived as laying out a string along which learners proceed in their own ways, exercising and improving their creative capacities and imaginations, and experiencing the joy of discovery.

Under these conceptions, in Dewey's words, industry must be changed "from a feudalistic to a democratic social order," and educational practice should be designed to encourage creativity, exploration, independence, cooperative work—much the opposite of what is happening today.

These ideas lead very naturally to a vision of society based on workers' control of productive institutions, as envisioned by nineteenth-century thinkers, notably Marx but also—less familiar—John Stuart Mill, who held that "the form of association, however, which if mankind continue to improve, must be expected to predominate is . . . the association of the labourers themselves on terms of equality, collectively owning the capital with which they carry on their operations, and working under managers electable and removable by themselves."[14] These should further be linked to community control within a framework of free association and federal organization, in the general style of a range of thought that includes, along with many anarchists, G. D. H. Cole's guild socialism and left anti-Bolshevik Marxism, and such current developments as the participatory economics and politics of Michael Albert, Robin Hahnel, Steven Shalom, and others, along with important work in theory and practice by the late Seymour Melman and his associates, and Gar Alperovitz's valuable recent contributions on the growth of worker-owned enterprise and cooperatives in the U.S. Rust Belt and elsewhere.

Dewey was a figure of the American mainstream. And, in fact, such ideas are deeply rooted in the American tradition. Pursuing them, we enter into the terrain of inspiring and often bitter struggle since the dawn of the industrial revolution in the mid-nineteenth century. The first serious scholarly study of the industrial worker in those years was by Norman Ware more than ninety years ago, still very much worth reading.[15] He reviews the hideous working conditions imposed on formerly independent craftsmen and farmers, as well as the "factory girls," young women from the farms working in the textile mills around Boston. But he focuses attention primarily on "the degradation suffered by the industrial worker," the loss "of status and independence," which could not be canceled even when there was material improvement. And on the radical capitalist "social revolution in which sovereignty in economic affairs passed from the community as a whole into the keeping of a special class" of masters, often remote from production, a group "alien to the producers." Ware shows that "for every protest against machine industry, there can be found a hundred against the new power of capitalist production and its discipline."

Workers were striking not just for bread but for roses, for dignity and independence, for their rights as free men and women. In their journals, they condemned "the blasting influence of monarchical principles on democratic soil," which will not be overcome until "they who work in the mills [will] own them," and sovereignty will return to free producers. Then they will no longer be "menials or the humble subjects of a foreign despot, [the absentee owners,] slaves in the strictest sense of the word [who] toil . . . for their masters." Rather, they will regain their status as "free American citizens."

The capitalist revolution instituted a crucial change from price to wage. When the producer sold his product for a price, Ware writes, "he retained his person. But when he came to sell his labor, he sold himself" and lost his dignity as a person as he became a slave—a "wage slave," the term commonly used. Some 170 years ago, a group of skilled workers in New York repeated the common view that a daily wage is a form of slavery and warned, perceptively, that a day might come when wage slaves "will so far forget what is due to manhood as to glory in a system forced on them by their necessity and in opposition to their feelings of independence and self-respect"—a day they hoped would be "far distant."

Labor activists warned of the new "spirit of the age: gain wealth, forgetting all but self." In sharp reaction to this demeaning spirit, the rising movements of working people and radical farmers, the most significant democratic popular movements in American history, were dedicated to solidarity and mutual aid[16]—a battle that is far from over, despite setbacks, often violent repression.

Apologists for the radical revolution of wage slavery argue that the worker should indeed glory in a system of free contracts, voluntarily undertaken. To them, Shelley had a response two centuries ago, in his great poem *Masque of Anarchy*, written after the Peterloo massacre, when British cavalry brutally attacked a peaceful gathering of tens of thousands calling for parliamentary reform.

We know what slavery is, Shelley wrote:

'Tis to work and have such pay
As just keeps life from day to day
In your limbs, as in a cell
For the tyrants' use to dwell,

. . .

'Tis to be slave in soul
And to hold no strong control
Over your own wills, but be
All that others make of ye.

The artisans and factory girls who struggled for dignity and independence and freedom might well have known Shelley's words. Observers noted that they had good libraries and were acquainted with standard works of English literature. Before mechanization and the wage system undermined independence and culture, Ware writes, a workshop would be a *lyceum*. Journeymen would hire boys to read to them while they worked. Their workplaces were "social businesses," with many opportunities for reading, discussion, and mutual improvement. Along with the factory girls, they bitterly complained of the attack on their culture. The same was true in England, a matter discussed in Jonathan Rose's monumental study of the reading habits of the working class of the day.[17] He contrasts "the passionate pursuit of knowledge by proletarian autodidacts" with the "pervasive philistinism of the British aristocracy." I am old enough to remember residues among working people in New York, who were immersed in the high culture of the day during the depths of the Great Depression.

I mentioned that Dewey and American workers held one version of democracy, with strong libertarian elements. But the dominant version has been a very different one. Its most instructive expression is at the progressive end of the mainstream intellectual spectrum, among good Wilson-FDR-Kennedy liberal intellectuals. Here are a few representative quotes.

The public are "ignorant and meddlesome outsiders [who] must be put in their place." Decisions must be in hands of the "intelligent minority [of] responsible men," who must be protected "from the trampling and roar of the bewildered herd." The herd does have a *function*. Its task is to lend its weight every few years to a choice among the responsible men, but apart from that its function is to be "spectators, not participants in action." All for their own good. We should not succumb to "democratic dogmatisms about men being the best judges of their own interests." They are not. We are: we, the responsible men. Therefore attitudes and opinions must be shaped and controlled. We must "regiment the minds of men the way an army regiments their bodies." In particular, we must introduce better discipline into the institutions responsible for "the indoctrination of the young." If that is achieved, then it will be possible to avoid such dangerous periods as the 1960s, "the time of troubles" in conventional elite discourse. We will be able to achieve more "moderation in democracy" and return to better days as when "Truman had been able to govern the country with the cooperation of a relatively small number of Wall Street lawyers and bankers."

These are quotes from icons of the liberal establishment: Walter Lippmann, Edward Bernays, Harold Lasswell, Samuel Huntington, and the Trilateral Commission, which largely staffed the Carter administration.[18]

This shriveled conception of democracy has solid roots. The founding fathers were much concerned about the hazards of democracy. In the debates of the Constitutional Convention, the main framer, James Madison, warned of these hazards. Naturally taking England as his model, he observed that "in England, at this day, if elections were open to all classes of people, the property of landed proprietors would be insecure. An agrarian law would soon take place," undermining the right to property. To ward off such injustice, "our government ought to secure the permanent interests of the country against innovation," arranging voting patterns and checks and balances so as "to protect the minority of the opulent against the majority," a prime task of decent government.[19]

The threat of democracy took on still larger proportions because of the likely increase in "the proportion of those who will labor under all the hardships of life, and secretly sigh for a more equal distribution of its blessings," as Madison anticipated. Perhaps influenced by Shays's Rebellion, he warned that "the equal laws of suffrage" might in time shift power into their hands. "No agrarian attempts have yet been made in this Country," he continued, "but symptoms of a levelling spirit ... have sufficiently appeared in a [*sic*] certain quarters to give warning of the future danger." For such reasons, Madison held that the Senate, the main seat of power in the constitutional system, "ought to come from and represent the wealth of the nation," the "more capable sett of men," and that other constraints on democratic rule should be instituted.

Madison's conundrum has continued to trouble government leaders. In 1958, for example, Secretary of State John Foster Dulles pondered the difficulties that the United States was facing in Latin America. He expressed his anxiety over the ability of domestic Communists "to get control of mass movements," which we "have no capacity to duplicate." Their advantage is that "the poor people are the ones they appeal to and they have always wanted to plunder the rich."[20] We somehow cannot rally them to the understanding that government must "protect the minority of the opulent from the majority." That inability to get our message across regularly compels us to resort to violence, contrary to our noblest principles and much to our sincere regret.

To succeed in "framing a system which we wish to last for ages," Madison held, it would be necessary to ensure that rulers will be drawn from the opulent minority. It would then be possible "to secure the rights of property agst. the danger from an equality of universality of suffrage, vesting compleate power over property in hands without a share in it." The phrase "rights of property" was regularly used to mean rights *to* property—that is, the rights of property owners. Many years later, in 1829, Madison reflected that those "without property, or the hope of acquiring it, cannot be expected to sympathize sufficiently with its rights, to be safe depositories of power over them." The solution was to ensure that society be fragmented, with limited public participation in the political arena, which is to be effectively in the hands of the wealthy and their agents. Scholarship generally agrees that "the Constitution was intrinsically an aristocratic document designed to check the democratic tendencies of the period," delivering power to a "better sort" of people and excluding "those who were not rich, well born, or prominent from exercising political power."[21]

In Madison's defense, we should remember that he "was—to depths that we today are barely able to imagine— an eighteenth-century gentleman of honor."[22] It was the "enlightened Statesman" and "benevolent philosopher" who, he anticipated, would hold the reins of power. Ideally "pure and noble," these "men of intelligence, patriotism, property and independent circumstances" would be a "chosen body of citizens, whose wisdom may best discern the true interests of their country, and whose patriotism and love of justice will be least likely to sacrifice it to temporary or partial considerations." They would thus "refine" and "enlarge" the "public views," guarding the public interest against the "mischiefs" of democratic majorities.

Not exactly the way it turned out.

The problem with democracy that Madison perceived had been recognized long before by Aristotle, in the first major work of political science: *Politics*. Reviewing a variety of political systems, he concluded that democracy was the best— or perhaps the least bad—but he recognized a flaw: the great mass of the poor could use their voting power to take the property of the rich, which would be unfair. Madison and Aristotle faced the same problem but selected opposite solutions: Aristotle advised reducing inequality, by what we would regard as welfare state measures; Madison felt that the answer was to reduce democracy.

The conflict between these conceptions of democracy goes back to the earliest modern democratic revolution, in seventeenth-century England, when a war raged between supporters of the king and of Parliament. The gentry, the "men of best quality" as they called themselves, were appalled by the rabble who did not want to be ruled by king or Parliament, but rather "by countrymen like ourselves, that know our wants." Their pamphlets explained that "it will never be a good world while knights and gentlemen make us laws, that are chosen for fear and do but oppress us, and do not know the people's sores."[23]

The essential nature of the conflict, which has far from ended, was captured simply by Thomas Jefferson in his last years, when he had serious concerns about the quality and fate of the democratic experiment. He distinguished between "aristocrats and democrats." The aristocrats are "those who fear and distrust the people, and wish to draw all powers from them into the hands of the higher classes." The democrats, in contrast, "identify with the people, have confidence in them, cherish and consider them as the honest & safe, altho' not the most wise depository of the public interest."[24]

The modern progressive intellectuals who seek to "put the public in its place" and are free of "democratic dogmatisms" about the capacity of the "ignorant and meddlesome outsiders" to enter the political arena are Jefferson's "aristocrats." Their basic views are widely held, though there are disputes about who should play the guiding role: "the technocratic and policy-oriented intellectuals" of the progressive "knowledge society," or bankers and corporate executives. Or in other versions, the Central Committee, or the Guardian Council of clerics. All are instances of the "political guardianship" that the genuine libertarian tradition seeks to dismantle and reconstruct from below, while also changing industry "from a feudalistic to a democratic social order" based on workers' control, respecting the dignity of the producer as a genuine person, not a tool in the hands of others, in accordance with a libertarian tradition that has deep roots—and, like Marx's old mole, is always burrowing close to the surface, always ready to peek through, sometimes in surprising and unexpected ways, seeking to bring about what seems to me at least to be a reasonable approximation to the common good.

THE TITLE FOR this chapter is drawn from Hume's observations about the man he called "the greatest and rarest genius that ever arose for the ornament and instruction of the species," Isaac Newton. In Hume's judgment, Newton's greatest achievement was that while he "seemed to draw the veil from some of the mysteries of nature, he shewed at the same time the imperfections of the mechanical philosophy; and thereby restored [Nature's] ultimate secrets to that obscurity, in which they ever did and ever will remain." On different grounds, others reached similar conclusions. Locke, for example, had observed that motion has effects "which we can in no way conceive motion able to produce"—as Newton had in fact demonstrated shortly before. Since we remain in "incurable ignorance of what we desire to know" about matter and its effects, Locke concluded, no "science of bodies [is] within our reach," and we can only appeal to "the arbitrary determination of that All-wise Agent who has made them to be, and to operate as they do, in a way wholly above our weak understandings to conceive."[1]

I think it is worth attending to such conclusions, the reasons for them, their aftermath, and what that history suggests about current concerns and inquiries in philosophy of mind.

The mechanical philosophy that Newton undermined is based on our commonsense understanding of the nature and interactions of objects, in large part genetically determined and, it appears, reflexively yielding such perceived properties as persistence of objects through time and space, and as a corollary their cohesion and continuity;[2] and causality through contact, a fundamental feature of intuitive physics, "body, as far as we can conceive, being able only to strike and affect body, and motion, according to the utmost reach of our ideas, being able to produce nothing but motion," as Locke plausibly characterized commonsense understanding of the world—the limits of our "ideas," in his sense. The theoretical counterpart was the materialist conception of the world that animated the seventeenth-century scientific revolution, the conception of the world as a machine, simply a far grander version of the automata that stimulated the imagination of thinkers of the time much in the way programmed computers do today: the remarkable clocks, the artifacts constructed by master artisans like Jacques de Vaucanson that imitated animal behavior and internal functions like digestion, the hydraulically activated machines that played instruments and pronounced words when triggered by visitors walking through the royal gardens. The mechanical philosophy aimed to dispense with forms flitting through the air, sympathies and antipathies, and other occult ideas, and to keep to what is firmly grounded in commonsense understanding and intelligible to it. As is well known, Descartes claimed to have explained the phenomena of the material world in mechanistic terms while also demonstrating that the mechanical philosophy is not all-encompassing, not reaching to the domain of mind—again pretty much in accord with the commonsense dualistic interpretation of oneself and the world around us.

I. Bernard Cohen observes that "there is testimony aplenty in Newton's *Principia* and *Opticks* to his general adherence to the Cartesian mechanical philosophy."[3] The word "general" is important. Newton was much influenced by the neo-Platonic and alchemical traditions, and also by the disturbing consequences of his own inquiries. For such reasons, he sometimes modified the stricter Cartesian dichotomy of matter and spirit, including in the latter category "the natural agencies responsible for the 'violent' motions of chemical and electrical action and even, perhaps, for accelerated motion in general," as Ernan McMullin shows in a careful analysis of the evolution of Newton's struggle with the paradoxes and conundrums he sought to resolve. In Newton's own words, "spirit" may be the cause of all movement in nature, including the "power of moving our body by our thoughts" and "the same power in other living creatures, [though] how this is done and by what laws we do not know. We cannot say that all nature is not alive."[4]

Going a step beyond, Locke added that we cannot say that nature does not think. In the formulation that has come down through history as "Locke's suggestion," he writes that "whether Matter may not be made by God to think is more than man can know. For I see no contradiction in it, that the first Eternal thinking Being, or Omnipotent Spirit, should, if he pleased, give to certain systems of created senseless matter, put together as he thinks fit, some degrees of sense, perception, and thought." Furthermore, just as God had added inconceivable effects to motion, it is "not much more remote from our comprehension to conceive that GOD can, if he pleases, superadd to matter a faculty of thinking, than that he should superadd to it another substance with a faculty of thinking." There is no warrant, then, for postulating a second substance whose essence is thought. And elsewhere, it "involves no contradiction [that God should] give to some parcels of matter, disposed as he thinks fit, a power of thinking and moving [which] might properly be called spirits, in contradistinction to unthinking matter," a view that he finds "repugnant to the *idea* of senseless matter" but that we cannot reject, given our incurable ignorance and the limits of our ideas (cognitive capacities). Having no intelligible concept of "matter" (body, etc.), we cannot dismiss the possibility of living or thinking matter, particularly after Newton undermined commonsense understanding.[5]

Locke's suggestion was taken up through the eighteenth century, culminating in the important work of Joseph Priestley, to which we will return. Hume, in the *Treatise*, reached the conclusion that "motion may be, and actually is, the cause of thought and perception," rejecting familiar arguments about absolute difference in kind and divisibility on the general grounds that "we are never sensible of any connexion betwixt causes and effects, and that 'tis only by our experience of their constant conjunction, we can arrive at any knowledge of this relation." In one or another form, it came to be recognized that since "thought, which is produced in the brain, cannot exist if this organ is wanting," and there is no longer a reason to question the thesis of thinking matter, "it is necessary to consider the brain as a special organ designed especially to produce [thought], as the stomach and the intestines are designed to operate the digestion, the liver to filter bile," and so on through the bodily organs. Just as foods enter the stomach and leave it with

> new qualities, [so] impressions arrive at the brain, through the nerves; they are then isolated and without coherence. The organ enters into action; it acts on them, and soon it sends them back changed into ideas, which the language of physiognomy and gesture, or the signs of speech and writing, manifest outwardly. We conclude then, with the same certainty, that the brain digests, as it were, the impressions, i.e., that organically it makes the secretion of thought.[6]

As Darwin put the matter succinctly, "Why is thought, being a secretion of the brain, more wonderful than gravity, a property of matter?"[7]

Qualifications aside, Newton did generally adhere to the mechanical philosophy but also showed its "imperfections," in fact demolished it, though to the end of his life he sought to find some way to account for the mystical principle of action at a distance that he was compelled to invoke to account for the most elementary phenomena of nature. Perhaps, he thought, there might be "a most subtle spirit which pervades and lies hid in all gross bodies," which will somehow yield a physical account of attraction and cohesion and offer some hope of rescuing an intelligible picture of the world.[8]

We should not lightly ignore the concerns of "the greatest and rarest genius that ever arose for the ornament and instruction of the species," or of Galileo and Descartes, or Locke and Hume. Or of Newton's most respected scientific contemporaries, who "unequivocally blamed [Newton] for leading science back into erroneous ways which it seemed to have definitely abandoned," E. J. Dijksterhuis writes in the classic study of the mechanistic world picture and its collapse as a substantive doctrine. Christiaan Huygens described Newton's principle of attraction as an "absurdity." Gottfried Leibniz argued that Newton was reintroducing occult ideas similar to the sympathies and antipathies of the much-ridiculed scholastic science and was offering no *physical* explanations for phenomena of the material world.[9]

Newton largely agreed with his scientific contemporaries. He wrote that the notion of action at a distance is "inconceivable." It is "so great an Absurdity, that I believe no Man who has in philosophical matters a competent Faculty of thinking, can ever fall into it."[10] By invoking it, we concede that we do not understand the phenomena of the material world. As McMullin observes, "By 'understand' Newton still meant what his critics meant: 'understand in mechanical terms of contact action.'"[11]

To take a contemporary analog, the absurd notion of action at a distance is as inconceivable as the idea that "mental states are states of the brain," a proposal "we do not really understand [because] we are still unable to form a conception of *how* consciousness arises in matter, even if we are certain that it does."[12] Similarly, Newton was unable to form a conception of how the simplest phenomena of nature could arise in matter—and they didn't, given his conception of matter, the natural theoretical version of commonsense understanding. Locke and others agreed, and Hume carried that failure of conceivability a long step beyond by concluding that Newton had restored these ultimate secrets of nature "to that obscurity, in which they ever did and ever will remain"—a stand that we may interpret, naturalistically, as a speculation about the limits of human cognitive capacities. In the light of history, there seems to be little reason to be concerned about the inconceivability of relating mind to brain, or about conceivability altogether, at least in inquiry into the nature of the world. Nor is there any reason for qualms about an "explanatory gap" between *the physical* and consciousness, beyond the unification concerns that arise throughout efforts to understand the world. And unless *the physical* is given some new post-Newtonian sense, there is even less reason for qualms about an "explanatory gap" than in cases where there is some clear sense to the assumed reduction base. The most extreme of such concerns, and perhaps the most significant for the subsequent development of the sciences, is the explanatory gap that Newton unearthed and left unresolved, possibly a permanent mystery for humans, as Hume conjectured.[13]

Science of course did not end with the collapse of the notion of body (material, physical, etc.). Rather, it was reconstituted in a radically new way, with questions of conceivability and intelligibility dismissed as demonstrating nothing except about human cognitive capacities, though that conclusion has taken a long time to become firmly established. Later stages of science introduced more "absurdities." The legitimacy of the steps is determined by criteria of depth of explanation and empirical support, not conceivability and intelligibility of the world that is depicted.

Thomas Kuhn suggests that "it does not, I think, misrepresent Newton's intentions as a scientist to maintain that he wished to write a *Principles of Philosophy* like Descartes [that is, true science] but that his inability to explain gravity forced him to restrict his subject to the *Mathematical Principles of Natural Philosophy*, [which] did not even pretend to explain why the universe runs as it does," leaving the question in obscurity. For such reasons, "it was 40 years before Newtonian physics firmly supplanted Cartesian physics, even in British universities," and some of the ablest physicists of the eighteenth century continued to seek a mechanical-corpuscular explanation of gravity—that is, what they took to be a *physical* explanation—as Newton did himself. In later years positivists reproached all sides of the debates "for their foolishness in clothing the mathematical formalism [of physical theory] with the 'gay garment' of a physical interpretation," a concept that had lost substantive meaning.[14]

Newton's famous phrase "I frame no hypotheses" appears in this context: recognizing that he had been unable to discover the *physical* cause of gravity, he left the question open. He adds that "to us it is enough that gravity does really exist, and act according to the laws which we have explained, and abundantly serves to account for all the motions of the celestial bodies, and of our sea." But while agreeing that his proposals were so absurd that no serious scientist could accept them, he defended himself from the charge that he was reverting to the mysticism of the Aristotelians. His principles, he argued, were not occult: "their causes only are occult"; or, he hoped, were yet to be discovered in physical terms, meaning mechanical terms. To derive general principles inductively from phenomena, he continued, "and afterwards to tell us how the properties of actions of all corporeal things follow from those manifest principles, would be a very great step in philosophy, though the causes of these principles were not yet discovered."[15]

To paraphrase with regard to the contemporary analog I mentioned, it "would be a very great step in science to account for mental aspects of the world in terms of manifest principles even if the causes of these principles were not yet discovered"—or to put the matter more appropriately, even if unification with other aspects of science had not been achieved. To learn more about mental aspects of the world— or chemical or electrical or other aspects—we should try to discover "manifest principles" that partially explain them, though their causes remain disconnected from what we take to be more fundamental aspects of science. The gap might have many reasons, among them, as has repeatedly been discovered, that the presumed reduction base was misconceived, including core physics.

Historians of science have recognized that Newton's reluctant intellectual moves set forth a new view of science in which the goal is not to seek ultimate explanations but to find the best theoretical account we can of the phenomena of experience and experiment. Newton's more limited goals were not entirely new. They have roots in an earlier scientific tradition that had abandoned the search for the "first springs of natural motions" and other natural phenomena, keeping to the more modest effort to develop the best theoretical account we can: what Richard Popkin calls the "constructive skepticism . . . formulated . . . in detail by [Marin] Mersenne and [Pierre] Gassendi," later in Hume's "mitigated skepticism." In this conception, Popkin continues, science proceeds by "doubting our abilities to find grounds for our knowledge, while accepting and increasing the knowledge itself" and recognizing that "the secrets of nature, of things-in-themselves, are forever hidden from us"—the "science without metaphysics . . . which was to have a great history in more recent times."[16]

As the impact of Newton's discoveries was slowly absorbed, such lowering of the goals of scientific inquiry became routine. Scientists abandoned the animating idea of the early scientific revolution: that the world will be intelligible to us. It is enough to construct intelligible explanatory theories, a radical difference. By the time we reach Bertrand Russell's *Analysis of Matter*, he dismisses the very idea of an intelligible world as "absurd" and repeatedly places the word "intelligible" in quotes to highlight the absurdity of the quest. Qualms about action at a distance were "little more than a prejudice," he writes. "If all the world consisted of billiard balls, it would be what is called 'intelligible'—i.e., it would never surprise us sufficiently to make us realize that we do not understand it."[17] But even without external surprise, we should recognize how little we understand the world and should also realize that it doesn't matter whether we can conceive of how the world works. In his classic introduction to quantum mechanics a few years later, Paul Dirac wrote that physical science no longer seeks to provide pictures of how the world works, that is, "a model functioning on essentially classical lines," but only seeks to provide a "way of looking at the fundamental laws which makes their self-consistency obvious." He was referring to the inconceivable conclusions of quantum physics but could just as readily have said that even the classical Newtonian models had abandoned the hope of rendering natural phenomena intelligible, the primary goal of the early modern scientific revolution, with its roots in commonsense understanding.[18]

It is useful to recognize how radical a shift it was to abandon the mechanical philosophy, and with it any scientific relevance of our commonsense beliefs and conceptions, except as a starting point and spur for inquiry. Galileo scholar Peter Machamer observes that by adopting the mechanical philosophy and initiating the modern scientific revolution, Galileo had "forged a new model of intelligibility for human understanding, [with] new criteria for coherent explanations of natural phenomena" based on the conception of the world as an elaborate machine. For Galileo, and leading figures in the early modern scientific revolution generally, true understanding requires a mechanical model, a device that an artisan could construct, hence intelligible to us. Thus Galileo rejected traditional theories of tides because we cannot "duplicate [them] by means of appropriate artificial devices."[19]

The model of intelligibility that reigned from Galileo through Newton and beyond has a corollary: when mechanism fails, understanding fails. The apparent inadequacies of mechanical explanation for cohesion, attraction, and other phenomena led Galileo finally to reject "the vain presumption of understanding everything." Worse yet, "there is not a single effect in nature . . . such that the most ingenious theorist can arrive at a complete understanding of it."[20] Galileo was formulating a very strong version of what Daniel Stoljar calls "the ignorance hypothesis" in his careful inquiry into the contemporary study of philosophical problems relating to consciousness, concluding that their origins are epistemic and that they are effectively overcome by invoking the ignorance hypothesis—which for Galileo, Newton, Locke, Hume, and others was more than a hypothesis and extended far beyond the problem of consciousness, encompassing the truths of nature quite generally.[21]

Though much more optimistic than Galileo about the prospects for mechanical explanation, Descartes, too, recognized the limits of our cognitive reach. Rule 8 of the *Regulae* reads: "If in the series of subjects to be examined we come to a subject of which our intellect cannot gain a good enough intuition, we must stop there; and we must not examine the other matters that follow, but must refrain from futile toil." Specifically, Descartes speculated that the workings of *res cogitans* may lie beyond human understanding. He thought that we may not "have intelligence enough" to understand the workings of mind, in particular, the normal use of language, with its creative aspects, his core example: the capacity of every human, but no beast-machine, to use language in ways appropriate to situations but not caused by them, and to formulate and express coherent thoughts without bound, perhaps "incited or inclined" to speak in certain ways by internal and external circumstances but not "compelled" to do so, as his followers put the matter.[22]

However, Descartes continued, even if the explanation of normal use of language and other forms of free and coherent choice of action lies beyond our cognitive grasp, that is no reason to question the authenticity of our experience. Quite generally, "free will" is "the noblest thing" we have, Descartes held: "there is nothing we comprehend more evidently and more perfectly," and "it would be absurd" to doubt something that "we comprehend intimately, and experience within ourselves" (that "the free actions of men [are] undetermined") merely because it conflicts with something else "which we know must be by its nature incomprehensible to us" ("divine preordination").[23]

Such thoughts about cognitive limits do not comport well with Descartes's occasional observation that human reason "is a universal instrument which can serve for all contingencies," whereas the organs of an animal or machine "have need of some special adaptation for any particular action." But let's put that aside and keep to the more reasonable conclusions about cognitive limits.

The creative use of language was a basis for what has been called the "epistemological argument" for mind-body dualism and also for the scientific inquiries of the Cartesians into the problem of "other minds"—much more sensible, I believe, than contemporary analogs, often based on misinterpretation of a famous paper of Alan Turing's, a topic that I will put aside.[24]

Desmond Clarke is accurate, I think, in concluding that "Descartes identified the use of language as the critical property that distinguishes human beings from other members of the animal kingdom and [that] he developed this argument in support of the real distinction of mind and matter." I think he is also persuasive in interpreting the general Cartesian project as primarily "natural philosophy" (science), an attempt to press mechanical explanation to its limits; and in regarding the *Meditations* "not as the authoritative expression of Descartes's philosophy, but as an unsuccessful attempt to reconcile his theologically suspect natural philosophy with an orthodox expression of scholastic metaphysics."[25] In pursuing his natural science, Descartes tried to show that mechanical explanation reached very far but came to an impassable barrier in the face of such mental phenomena as the creative use of language. He therefore, quite properly, adopted the standard scientific procedure of seeking some new principles to account for such mental phenomena—a quest that lost one primary motivation when mechanical explanation was demonstrated to fail for everything.

Clarke argues that "Descartes's dualism was an expression of the extent of the theoretical gap between [Cartesian physics] and the descriptions of mental life that we formulate from the first person perspective of our own thinking." The gap therefore results from Descartes's "impoverished concept of matter" and can be overcome by "including new theoretical entities in one's concept of matter."[26] Whether the latter speculation is correct or not, it does not quite capture the deficiencies of classical science from Galileo through Newton and beyond. The underlying concept of matter and motion—based on conceivability, intelligibility and commonsense understanding—had to be abandoned, and science had to proceed on an entirely new course in investigating the simplest phenomena of motion, and all other aspects of the world, including mental life.

Despite the centrality of the creative use of language to Cartesian science, it was only one illustration of the general problem of will, and choice of appropriate action, which remains as mysterious to us as it was to seventeenth-century scientists, so it seems to me, despite sophisticated arguments to the contrary. The problems are hardly even on the scientific agenda. There has been very valuable work about how an organism executes a plan for integrated motor action—say, how a person reaches for a cup on the table. But no one even raises the question of why this plan is executed rather than some other one, apart from the very simplest organisms and special circumstances of motivation. Much the same is true even for visual perception. Cognitive neuroscientists Nancy Kanwisher and Paul Downing reviewed research on a problem posed in 1850 by Hermann von Helmholtz: "even without moving our eyes, we can focus our attention on different objects at will, resulting in very different perceptual experiences of the same visual field." The phrase "at will" points to an area beyond serious empirical inquiry, still the mystery it was for Newton at the end of his life when he continued to seek some "subtle spirit" that lies hidden in all bodies and that might, without "absurdity," account for their properties of attraction and repulsion, along with the nature and effects of light, sensation, and the way "members of animal bodies move at the command of the will"—all comparable mysteries for Newton, perhaps even beyond our understanding.[27]

It has become standard practice in recent years to describe the problem of consciousness as "the hard problem," others being within our grasp, now or down the road. I think there are reasons for some skepticism, particularly when we recognize how sharply understanding declines beyond the simplest systems of nature. To illustrate with a few examples, a review article by Eric Kandel and Larry Squire on the current state of efforts aimed at "breaking down scientific barriers to the study of brain and mind" concludes that "the neuroscience of higher cognitive processes is only beginning."[28] Charles Gallistel points out that "we clearly do not understand how the nervous system computes," or even "the foundations of its ability to compute," even for "the small set of arithmetic and logical operations that are fundamental to any computation." Reviewing the remarkable computational capacities of insects, he concludes that it is a mistake to suppose that the nervous system does not carry out complex symbolic computations on grounds of "our inability, as yet to understand how the nervous system computes at the cellular and molecular level. . . . We do not know what processes belong to the basic instruction set of the nervous system—the modest number of elementary operations built into the hardware of any computing device."[29] Semir Zeki, who is optimistic about the prospects for bringing the brain sciences to bear even on creativity in the visual arts, nevertheless reminds us that "how the brain combines the responses of specialized cells to indicate a continuous vertical line is a mystery that neurology has not yet solved," or even how one line is differentiated from others or from the visual surround. Basic traditional questions are not even on the research agenda, and even simple ones that might be within reach remain baffling.[30]

It is common to assert that "the mental is the neurophysiological at a higher level." To entertain the idea makes sense, but for the present, only as a guide to inquiry, without much confidence about what "the neurophysiological" will prove to be. Similarly, it is premature to hold that "it is empirically evident that states of consciousness are the necessary consequence of neuronal activity." Too little is understood about the functioning of the brain.[31]

History also suggests caution. In early modern science, the nature of motion was the "hard problem." "Springing or

Elastic Motions" is the "hard rock in Philosophy," Sir William Petty observed, proposing ideas resembling those soon developed much more richly by Newton. The "hard problem" was that bodies that seem to our senses to be at rest are in a "violent" state, with "a strong endeavor to fly off or recede from one another," in Robert Boyle's words. The problem, he felt, is as obscure as "the Cause and Nature" of gravity, thus supporting his belief in "an intelligent Author or Disposer of Things." Even the skeptical Newtonian Voltaire argued that the ability of humans to "produce a movement" where there was none shows that "there is a God who gave movement" to matter, and "so far are we from conceiving what matter is" that we do not even know if there is any "solid matter in the universe." Locke relinquished to divine hands "the gravitation of matter towards matter, by ways, inconceivable to me." Kant rephrased the "hard problem," arguing that to reach his conclusions, Newton was compelled to tacitly "assume that all matter exercises this motive force [of universal attraction] simply as matter and by its essential nature"; by rejecting the assumption, he was "at variance with himself," caught in a contradiction. Newton therefore did not, as he claimed, really leave "the physicists full freedom to explain the possibility of such attraction as they might find good, without mixing up his propositions with their play of hypotheses." Rather, "the concept of matter is reduced to nothing but moving forces. . . . The attraction essential to all matter is an immediate action of one matter on another across empty space," a notion that would have been anathema to the great figures of seventeenth-century science, "such Masters, as the Great Huygenius, and the incomparable Mr. Newton," in Locke's words.[32]

The "hard problems" of the day were not solved; rather they were abandoned, as, over time, science turned to its more modest post-Newtonian course. Friedrich Lange, in his classic nineteenth-century history of materialism, observed that we have

> so accustomed ourselves to the abstract notion of forces, or rather to a notion hovering in a mystic obscurity between abstraction and concrete comprehension, that we no longer find any difficulty in making one particle of matter act upon another without immediate contact, . . . through void space without any material link. From such ideas the great mathematicians and physicists of the seventeenth century were far removed. They were all in so far genuine Materialists in the sense of ancient Materialism that they made immediate contact a condition of influence.

This transition over time is "one of the most important turning-points in the whole history of Materialism," depriving the doctrine of much significance, if any at all. Newton not only joined the great scientists of his day in regarding "the now prevailing theory of *actio in distans* . . . simply as absurd, [but] also felt himself obliged, in the year 1717, in the preface to the second edition of his 'Optics,' to protest expressly against [the] view" of his followers who "went so far as to declare gravity to be a fundamental force of matter," requiring no "further mechanical explanation from the collision of imponderable particles." Lange concludes that "the course of history has eliminated this unknown material cause [that so troubled Newton], and has placed the mathematical law itself in the rank of physical causes." Hence "what Newton held to be so great an absurdity that no philosophic thinker could light upon it, is prized by posterity as Newton's great discovery of the harmony of the universe!"[33] The conclusions are commonplace in the history of science. Fifty years ago, Alexandre Koyré observed that despite his unwillingness to accept the conclusion, Newton had demonstrated that "a purely materialistic pattern of nature is utterly impossible (and a purely materialistic or mechanistic physics, such as that of Lucretius or of Descartes, is utterly impossible, too)"; his mathematical physics required the "admission into the body of science of incomprehensible and inexplicable 'facts' imposed up on us by empiricism," by what is observed and our conclusions from these observations.[34]

George Coyne describes it as "paradoxical that the rise of materialism as a philosophy in the 17th and 18th centuries is attributed to the birth of modern science, when in reality matter as a workable concept had been eliminated from scientific discourse" with the collapse of the mechanical philosophy.[35] Also paradoxical is the influence of Gilbert Ryle's ridicule of the "ghost in the machine," quite apart from the accuracy of his rendition of the Cartesian concepts. It was the machine that Newton exorcised, leaving the ghost intact. The "hard problem" of the materialists disappeared, and there has been little noticeable progress in addressing other "hard problems" that seemed no less mysterious to Descartes, Newton, Locke, and other leading figures.

The third English edition of Lange's much expanded history of materialism appeared in 1925 with an introduction by Bertrand Russell, who shortly after published *Analysis of*

Matter. Developing his neutral monism, Russell carried further seventeenth- and eighteenth-century skepticism about matter, and recognition of the plausibility (or for some necessity) of thinking matter. Russell held that there are "three grades of certainty. The highest grade belongs to my own percepts; the second grade to the percepts of other people; the third to events which are not percepts of anybody," constructions of the mind established in the course of efforts to make sense of what we perceive. "A piece of matter is a logical structure composed of [such] events," he therefore concluded. We know nothing of the "intrinsic character" of such mentally constructed entities, so there is "no ground for the view that percepts cannot be physical events." For science to be informative, it cannot be restricted to structural knowledge of such logical properties. Rather, "the world of physics [that we construct] must be, in some sense, continuous with the world of our perceptions, since it is the latter which supplies the evidence for the laws of physics." The percepts that are required for this task—perhaps just meter-readings, Arthur Eddington had argued shortly before—"are not known to have any intrinsic character which physical events cannot have, since we do not know of any intrinsic character which could be incompatible with the logical properties that physics assigns to physical events." Accordingly, "what are called 'mental' events . . . are part of the material of the physical world." Physics itself seeks only to discover "the causal skeleton of the world, [while studying] percepts only in their cognitive aspect; their other aspects lie outside its purview"—though we recognize their existence, at the highest grade of certainty in fact.[36]

The basic conundrum recalls a classical dialogue between the intellect and the senses, in which the intellect says that color, sweetness, and the like are only convention while in reality there are only atoms and the void, and the senses reply: "Wretched mind, from us you are taking the evidence by which you would overthrow us? Your victory is your own fall."[37]

To illustrate his conclusion, Russell asks us to consider a blind physicist who knows the whole of physics but does not have "the knowledge which [sighted] men have" about, say, the quality of the color blue. In their review of related issues, Daniel Stoljar and Yujin Nagasawa call this the "knowledge intuition," as distinct from the "knowledge argument," presented in the resurrection of Russell's example by Frank Jackson: in this case, the physicist (Mary) "learns everything there is to know about the physical nature of the world" while confined to a black-and-white room but when released "will learn what it is like to see something red."[38]

There is a substantial literature seeking to evade the argument. One popular though contested proposal is that what Mary lacks is not the knowledge of the world that we have but a range of abilities, a species of "knowing how." That seems unhelpful, in part because there is an irreducible cognitive element in "knowing how," which goes beyond abilities; but also for the kinds of reasons that Hume discussed in connection with moral judgments. Since these, he observed, are unbounded in scope and applicable to new situations, they must be based on a finite array of general principles (which are, furthermore, part of our nature though they are beyond the "original instincts" shared with animals). The knowledge that *we* have but Mary lacks is a body of knowledge that does not fall within the knowing-how/knowing-that dichotomy: it is knowledge *of*—knowledge of rules and principles that yield unbounded capacities to act appropriately. All this is for the most part unconscious and inaccessible to consciousness, as in the case of knowledge of the rules of language, vision, and the like. Such conclusions have been rejected as a matter of principle by Willard Van Orman Quine, John Searle, and many others but not convincingly or even coherently, I think.[39]

Russell's knowledge intuition led him to conclude that physics has limits: experience in general lies "outside its purview" apart from cognitive aspects that provide empirical evidence, though along with other mental events, experience is "part of the material of the physical world," a phrase that seems to mean no more than "part of the world." We must have "an interpretation of physics which gives a due place to perceptions," Russell held, or it has no empirical basis. Jackson's knowledge argument leads him to the conclusion that "physicalism is false." Or in a later version, that to be valid "materialism [as] a metaphysical doctrine" must incorporate "the psychological story about our world"; the "story about our world told purely in physical terms [must] enable one to deduce the phenomenal nature of psychological states."[40] But that is uninformative until some clear concept of physicalism/materialism is offered. Classical interpretations having vanished, the notions of body, material, physical are hardly more than honorific designations for what is more or less understood at some particular moment in time, with flexible boundaries and no guarantee that there will not be radical revision ahead, even at its core. If so, the knowledge argument only shows (with Russell) that humanly constructed physics has limits, or that Mary did not know all of physics (she had not drawn the right conclusions from Eddington's meter readings).

To resurrect something that resembles a "mind-body problem," it would be necessary to characterize *physicalism* (*matter*, etc.) in some post-Newtonian fashion, or to argue that the problem arises even if the concepts are abandoned. Both approaches have been pursued. I will return to current examples. An alternative approach is to dismiss the mind-body problem, and to approach the knowledge intuition/argument as a problem of the natural sciences. Rephrasing Russell's thought experiment, we might say that, like all animals, we have internal capacities that reflexively provide us with what ethologists called an *Umwelt*, a world of experience, different for us and for bees—in fact, differing among humans, depending on what they understand. That's why radiology is a medical specialty. Galileo saw the moons of Jupiter through his primitive telescope, but those he sought to convince could see only magnification of terrestrial objects, and took his telescope to be a conjuring trick (at least if Paul Feyerabend's reconstruction of the history is correct). What I hear as noise is perceived as music by my teenage grandchildren, at a fairly primitive level of perceptual experience. And so on quite generally.

Being reflective creatures, unlike others, we go on to seek to gain a deeper understanding of the phenomena of experience. These exercises are called myth, or magic, or philosophy, or science. They reveal not only that the world of experience is itself highly intricate and variable, resulting from the interaction of many factors, but also that the modes of interpretation that intuitive common sense provides do not withstand analysis, so that the goals of science must be lowered in the manner recognized in post-Newtonian science. From this point of view, there is no objective science from a third-person perspective, just various first-person perspectives, matching closely enough among humans so that a large range of agreement can be reached, with diligence and cooperative inquiry. Being inquisitive as well as reflective creatures, if we can construct a degree of theoretical understanding in some domain, we try to unify it with other branches of inquiry, reduction being one possibility but not the only one.

We can anticipate that our quest might fail, for one reason, because our basically shared capacities of understanding and explanation have limits—a truism that is sometimes thoughtlessly derided as "mysterianism," though not by Descartes and Hume, among others. It could be that these innate cognitive capacities do not lead us beyond some understanding of Russell's causal skeleton of the world (and enough about perception to incorporate evidence within this mental construction), and it is an open question how much of that can be attained. In principle, the limits could become topics of empirical inquiry into the nature of what we might call "the science-forming faculty," another "mental organ." These are interesting topics, but the issues are distinct from the traditional mind-body problem, which evaporated after Newton, or from the question of how mental aspects of the world, including direct experience, relate to the brain, one of the many problems of unification that arise in the sciences.

In brief, if we are biological organisms, not angels, much of what we seek to understand might lie beyond our cognitive limits—maybe a true understanding of anything, as Galileo concluded, and Newton in a certain sense demonstrated. That cognitive reach has limits is not only a truism but also a fortunate one: if there were no limits to human intelligence, it would lack internal structure and would therefore have no scope: we could achieve nothing by inquiry. The basic points were expressed clearly by Charles Sanders Peirce in his discussion of the need for innate endowment that "puts a limit upon admissible hypotheses" if knowledge is to be acquired.[41] Similarly if a zygote had no further genetic instructions constraining its developmental path, it would at best grow into a creature formed solely by physical law, like a snowflake, nothing viable.

We might think of the natural sciences as a kind of chance convergence between our cognitive capacities and what is more or less true of the natural world. There is no reason to believe that humans can solve every problem they pose or even that they can formulate the right questions; they may simply lack the conceptual tools, just as rats cannot deal with a prime number maze.

Russell's general conclusions seem to me on the right track. The formulation can be improved, I think, by simply dropping the words "matter" and "physical." Since the Newtonian revolution, we speak of the "physical" world much as we speak of the "real" truth: for emphasis, but adding nothing. We can distinguish various aspects of the world—say chemical, electrical, experiential and the rest—and we can then inquire into their underlying principles and their relations with other systems, problems of unification.

Suppose we adopt the "mitigated skepticism" that was warranted after Newton, if not before. For the theory of mind, that means following Gassendi's advice in *Objections*. He argued that Descartes had at most shown "the perception of the existence of mind, [but] fail[ed] to reveal its nature." It is necessary to proceed as we would in seeking to discover "a conception of Wine superior to the vulgar," by investigating how it is constituted and the laws that determine its functioning. Similarly, he urged Descartes, "it is incumbent on you, to examine yourself by a certain chemicallike labor, so that you can determine and demonstrate to us your internal substance"[42]—and that of others.

The theory of mind can be pursued in many ways, like other branches of science, with an eye to eventual unification, whatever form it may take, if any. That is the task that Hume undertook when he investigated what he called "the science of human nature," seeking "the secret springs and principles, by which the human mind is actuated in its operations," including those "parts of [our] knowledge" that are derived from "the original hand of nature," an enterprise he compared to Newton's; essentially what in contemporary literature is termed "naturalization of philosophy" or "epistemology naturalized." Gassendi's recommended course was in fact being pursued in the "cognitive revolution" of the seventeenth century by British neoplatonists and continental philosophers of language and mind and has been taken up with renewed vigor in recent years, but I'll put that matter aside.[43]

Chemistry itself quite explicitly pursued this course. The eighteenth-century chemist Joseph Black recommended that "chemical affinity be received as a first principle, which we cannot explain any more than Newton could explain gravitation, and let us defer accounting for the laws of affinity, till we have established such a body of doctrine as he has established concerning the laws of gravitation." Being yet "very far from the knowledge of first principles," chemical science should be "analytical, like Newton's *Optics*, in the form of a general law, at the very end of our induction, as the reward of our labour." The course he outlined is the one that was actually followed, as chemistry established a rich body of doctrine, its "triumphs . . . built on no reductionist foundation but rather achieved in isolation from the newly emerging science of physics," historian of chemistry Arnold Thackray observes. Newton and his followers did attempt to "pursue the thoroughly Newtonian and reductionist task of uncovering the general mathematical laws which govern all chemical behavior" and to develop a principled science of chemical mechanisms based on physics and its concepts of interactions among "the ultimate permanent particles of matter." But the Newtonian program was undercut by John Dalton's "astonishingly successful weight-quantification of chemical units," Thackray continues, shifting "the whole area of philosophical debate among chemists from that of chemical *mechanisms* (the *why*? of reaction) to that of chemical *units* (the *what*? and *how much*?)," a theory that "was profoundly antiphysicalist and anti-Newtonian in its rejection of the unity of matter, and its dismissal of short-range forces." "Dalton's ideas were chemically successful. Hence they have enjoyed the homage of history, unlike the philosophically more coherent, if less successful, reductionist schemes of the Newtonians."[44]

Adopting contemporary terminology, we might say that Dalton disregarded the explanatory gap between chemistry and physics by ignoring the underlying physics, much as post-Newtonian physicists disregarded the explanatory gap between Newtonian dynamics and the mechanical philosophy by ignoring (and in this case rejecting) the latter, though it was self-evident to commonsense understanding. That has often been the course of science since, though not without controversy and sharp criticism, often later recognized to have been seriously misguided.

Well into the twentieth century, prominent scientists interpreted the failure of reduction of chemistry to physics as a critically important explanatory gap, showing that chemistry provides "merely classificatory symbols that summarized the observed course of a reaction," to quote William Brock's standard history. August Kekulé, whose structural chemistry was an important step toward eventual unification of chemistry and physics, doubted that "absolute constitutions of organic molecules could ever be given"; his models and analysis of valency were to have an instrumental interpretation only, as calculating devices. Antoine Lavoisier before him believed that "the number and nature of elements [is] an unsolvable problem, capable of an infinity of solutions none of which probably accord with Nature"; "It seems extremely probable that we know nothing at all about . . . [the] . . . indivisible atoms of which matter is composed," and never will, he believed. Kekulé seems to be saying that there isn't a problem to be solved; the structural formulas are useful or not, but there is no truth of the matter. Large parts of physics were understood the same way. Henri Poincaré went so far as to say that we adopt the molecular theory of gases only because we are familiar with the game of billiards. Ludwig Boltzmann's scientific biographer speculates that he committed suicide because of his failure to convince the scientific community to regard his theoretical account of these matters as more than a calculating system—ironically, shortly after Albert Einstein's work on Brownian motion and broader issues had convinced physicists of the reality of the entities he postulated. Niels Bohr's model of the atom was also regarded as lacking "physical reality" by eminent scientists. In the 1920s, America's first Nobel Prize–winning chemist dismissed talk about the real nature of chemical bonds as metaphysical "twaddle": they are nothing more than "a very crude method of representing certain known facts about chemical reactions, a mode of representation" only, because the concept could not be reduced to physics. The rejection of that skepticism by a few leading scientists, whose views were condemned at the time as a conceptual absurdity, paved the way for the eventual unification of chemistry and physics, with Linus Pauling's quantum-theoretic account of the chemical bond seventy years ago.[45]

In 1927, Russell observed that chemical laws "cannot at present be reduced to physical laws,"[46] an observation that was found to be misleading: the words "at present" turned out to understate the matter. Chemical laws could not ever be reduced to physical laws, because the conception of physical laws was erroneous. The perceived explanatory gap was never filled. It was necessary, once again, to dismiss as irrelevant the notion of "conceivability" and "intelligibility of the world," in favor of the mitigated skepticism of methodological naturalism: seeking to increase our knowledge while keeping an open mind about the possibility of reduction.

There are fairly clear parallels to contemporary discussion of language and mind, and some lessons that can be drawn.

The study of insect symbolic representation, organization of motor behavior, mammalian vision, human language, moral judgment, and other topics is in each case well advised to follow Joseph Black's prescription. If these inquiries succeed in developing a "body of doctrine" that accounts for elements of insect navigation, or the rule that image motions are interpreted (if other rules permit) as rigid motions in three dimensions, or that displacement operations in language observe locality principles, and so on, that should be regarded as normal science, even if unification with neurophysiology has not been achieved—and might not be for a variety of possible reasons, among them that the expected "reduction base" is misconceived and has to be modified. Needless to say, the brain sciences are not as firmly established as basic physics was a century ago, or as the mechanical philosophy was in Newton's day. It is also pointless to insist on doctrines about accessibility to consciousness: even if they could be given a coherent formulation, they would have no bearing on the "physical reality" of the rigidity principle or locality conditions. We should understand enough by now to dismiss the interpretation of theoretical accounts as no more than a way of "representing certain known facts about [behavior], a mode of representation" only—a critique commonly leveled against theories of higher mental faculties, though not insect computation, another illustration of the methodological dualism that is so prevalent in critical discussion of inquiry into language and mind.[47]

It is also instructive to observe the re-emergence of much earlier insights, though divorced from their grounding in the collapse of traditional physicalism. Thus we read today of the thesis of the new biology that "things mental, indeed minds, are emergent properties of brains, [though] these emergences are . . . produced by principles that . . . we do not yet understand," according to neuroscientist Vernon Mountcastle, formulating the guiding theme of a collection of essays that review the results of the Decade of the Brain, which ended the twentieth century. The phrase "we do not *yet* understand" might well suffer the same fate as Russell's similar comment about chemistry seventy years earlier. Many other prominent scientists and philosophers have presented essentially the same thesis as an "astonishing hypothesis" of the new biology, a "radical" new idea in the philosophy of mind, "the bold assertion that mental phenomena are entirely natural and caused by the neurophysiological activities of the brain," opening the door to novel and promising inquiries, a rejection of Cartesian mind-body dualism, and so on.[48] In fact, all reiterate, in virtually the same words, formulations of centuries ago, after the traditional mind-body problem became unformulable with the disappearance of the only coherent notion of body (physical, material, etc.)—for example, Joseph Priestley's conclusion that properties "termed mental" reduce somehow to "the organical structure of the brain,"[49] stated in different words by Hume, Darwin, and many others, and almost inescapable, it would seem, after the collapse of the mechanical philosophy.

Priestley's important work was the culmination of a century of reflections on Locke's speculation, and their most elaborate development.[50] He made it clear that his conclusions about thinking matter followed directly from the collapse of any serious notion of *body*, or *matter*, or *physical*:

The principles of the Newtonian philosophy were no sooner known, than it was seen how few in comparison, of the phenomena of Nature were owing to solid matter, and how much to powers which were only supposed to accompany and surround the solid parts of matter.... Now when solidity had apparently so very little to do in the system, it is really a wonder that it did not occur to philosophers sooner ... that there might be no such thing in Nature.

There is, then, no longer any reason to suppose that "the principle of thought or sensation [is] incompatible with matter," Priestley concluded. Accordingly, "the whole argument for an immaterial thinking principle in man, on this supposition, falls to the ground; matter, destitute of what has hitherto been called solidity, being no more incompatible with sensation and thought than that substance which without knowing anything farther about it, we have been used to call immaterial." The powers of sensation, perception, and thought reside in "a certain organized system of matter, [and] necessarily exist in, and depend upon, such a system." It is true that "we have a very imperfect idea of what the power of perception is," and that we may never attain a "clear idea," but "this very ignorance ought to make us cautious in asserting with what other properties it may, or may not, exist." Only a "precise and definite knowledge of the nature of perception and thought can authorize any person to affirm whether they may not belong to an extended substance which also has the properties of attraction and repulsion." Our ignorance provides no warrant for supposing that sensation and thought are incompatible with post-Newtonian matter. "In fact, there is the same reason to conclude, that the powers of sensation and thought are the necessary result of a particular organization, as that sound is the necessary result of a particular concussion of the air." And in a later discussion, "In my opinion there is just the same reason to conclude that the brain *thinks*, as that it is *white*, and *soft*."[51]

Priestley criticizes Locke for being hesitant in putting forth his speculation about thinking matter, since the conclusion follows so directly from "the universally accepted rules of philosophizing such as are laid down by Sir Isaac Newton." He urges that we abandon the methodological dualism that deters us from applying to thought and sensation the rules that we follow "in our inquiries into the causes of particular appearances in nature" and expresses his hope "that when this is plainly pointed out the inconsistency of our conduct cannot fail to strike us and be the means of inducing" philosophers to apply the same maxim to investigation of mental aspects of the world that they do in other domains—a hope that has yet to be realized, I think.[52]

Priestley clearly "wished the disappearance of solid matter to signal an end to matter-spirit dualism," Thackray writes. And with it an end to any reason to question the thesis of thinking matter.[53] In John Yolton's words, Priestley's conclusion was "not that all reduces to matter, but rather that the kind of matter on which the two-substance view is based does not exist," and "with the altered concept of matter, the more traditional ways of posing the question of the nature of thought and of its relations to the brain do not fit. We have to think of a complex organized biological system with properties the traditional doctrine would have called mental *and* physical."[54] Priestley's conclusions are essentially those reached by

Eddington and Russell, and developed in recent years particularly by Galen Strawson and Daniel Stoljar, in ways to which we return.

Reviewing the development of Locke's suggestion in England through the eighteenth century, Yolton observes that "Priestley's fascinating suggestions were not taken up and extended; they were hardly even perceived as different from earlier versions of materialism. The issues raised by Locke's suggestion of thinking matter . . . played themselves out through the century, but no one gave the emerging view of man as one substance—foreshadowed by Priestley—a systematic articulation."[55] This conclusion remains largely true, even for simple organisms, if we interpret it as referring to the unification problem.

Having argued that the mind-body problem disappears when we follow the "principles of the Newtonian philosophy," Priestley turns to confronting efforts to reconstitute something that resembles the problem, even after one of its terms—body (matter, etc.)—no longer has a clear sense. The first is "the difficulty of conceiving how thought can arise from matter, . . . an argument that derives all its force from our ignorance," he writes, and has no force unless there is a demonstration that they are "absolutely incompatible with one another." Priestley was not troubled by qualms arising from ignorance, rightly I think, any more than scientists should have been concerned about irreducibility of the mysterious properties of matter and motion to the mechanical philosophy, or in more modern times, about the inability to reduce chemistry to an inadequate physics until the 1930s, to take two significant moments from the history of science.

A common objection today is that such ideas invoke an unacceptable form of "radical emergence," unlike the emergence of liquids from molecules, where the properties of the liquid can in some reasonable sense be regarded as inhering in the molecules. In Nagel's phrase, "we can *see* how liquidity is the logical result of the molecules 'rolling around on each other' at the microscopic level," though "nothing comparable is to be expected in the case of neurons" and consciousness.[56]

Also taking liquidity as a paradigm, Strawson argues extensively that the notion of emergence is intelligible only if we interpret it as "total dependence": if "some part or aspect of Y [hails] from somewhere else," then we cannot say that Y is "emergent from X." We can speak intelligibly about emergence of Y-phenomena from non-Y-phenomena only if the non-Y-phenomena at the very least are "somehow *intrinsically suited* to constituting" the X-phenomena; there must be "something about X's nature in virtue of which" they are "so suited." "It is built into the notion of emergence that emergence cannot be brute in the sense of there being no reason in the nature of things why the emerging thing is as it is." This is Strawson's *No-Radical Emergence Thesis*, from which he draws the panpsychic conclusion that "experiential reality cannot possibly emerge from wholly and utterly non-experiential reality." The basic claim, which he highlights, is that "if it really is true that Y is emergent from X then it must be the case that Y is in some sense wholly dependent on X and X alone, so that all features of Y trace intelligibly back to X." Here "intelligible" is a metaphysical rather than an epistemic notion, meaning "intelligible to God": there must be an explanation in the nature of things, though we may not be able to attain it.[57]

Priestley, it seems, would reject Nagel's qualms while accepting Strawson's formulation, but without drawing the panpsychic conclusion. It should be noted that the molecule-liquid example, commonly used, is not a very telling one. We also cannot conceive of a liquid turning into two gases by electrolysis, and there is no intuitive sense in which the properties of water, bases, and acids inhere in hydrogen or oxygen or other atoms. Furthermore, the whole matter of conceivability seems to be irrelevant, whether it is brought up in connection with the effects of motion that Newton and Locke found inconceivable, or the irreducible principles of chemistry, or mind-brain relations. There is something about the nature of hydrogen and oxygen "in virtue of which they are intrinsically suited to constituting water," so the sciences discovered after long labors, providing reasons "in the nature of things why the emerging thing is as it is." What seemed "brute emergence" was assimilated into science as ordinary emergence—not, to be sure, of the liquidity variety, relying on conceivability. I see no strong reason why matters should necessarily be different in the case of experiential and nonexperiential reality, particularly given our ignorance of the latter, stressed from Newton and Locke to Priestley, developed by Russell, and arising again in recent discussion.

Priestley then considers the claim that mind "cannot be material because it is influenced by reasons." To this he responds that since "reasons, whatever they may be, do ultimately move matter, there is certainly much less difficulty in conceiving that they may do this in consequence of their being the affection of some material substance, than upon the hypothesis of their belonging to a substance that has no common property with matter"—not the way it would be put to-day, but capturing essentially the point of contemporary discussion leading some to revive panpsychism. But contrary to the contemporary revival,[58] Priestley rejects the conclusion that consciousness "cannot be annexed to the whole brain as a system, while the individual particles of which it consists are separately unconscious." That "a certain quantity of nervous system is necessary to such complex ideas and affections as belong to the human mind; and the idea of self, or the feeling that corresponds to the pronoun I," he argues, "is not essentially different from other complex ideas, that of our country for example." Similarly, it should not perplex us more than the fact that "life should be the property of an entirely animal system, and not the separate parts of it," or that sound cannot "result from the motion of a single particle" of air. We should recognize "that the term self denotes that substance which is the seat of that particular set of sensations and ideas of which those that are then recollected make a part, as distinct from other substances which are the seat of similar sets of sensations and ideas": and "it is high time to abandon these random hypotheses, and to form our conclusions with respect to the faculties of the mind, as well as the properties and powers of matter, by an attentive observation of facts and cautious inferences from them," adopting the Newtonian style of inquiry while dismissing considerations of commonsense plausibility. That seems to be a reasonable stance.

Priestley urges that we also dismiss arguments based on "vulgar phraseology" and "vulgar apprehensions," as in the quest for an entity of the world picked out by the term *me* when I speak of "my body," with its hint of dualism. "According to this merely verbal argument," Priestley observes, "there ought to be something in man besides all the parts of which he consists," something beyond both soul and body, as when "a man says I devote my soul and body," the pronoun allegedly denoting something beyond body and spirit that "makes the devotion." In Rylean terms, phrases of common usage may be "systematically misleading expressions," a lively concern at the time, based on a centuries-old tradition of inquiry into the ways surface grammatical form disguise actual meaning. Like Priestley, Thomas Reid argued that failure to attend "to the distinction between the operations of the mind and the objects of these operations" is a source of philosophical error, as in interpreting the phrase "I have an idea" on the model of "I have a diamond," when we should understand it to mean something like "I am thinking." In an earlier discussion, the Encyclopedist César Chesneau du Marsais, using the same and many other examples, warned against the error of taking nouns to be "names of real objects that exist independently of our thought." The language, then, gives no license for supposing that such words as "idea," "concept," or "image" stand for "real objects," let alone "perceptible objects."[59] For similar reasons, Priestley argues that "nothing surely can be inferred from such phraseology as ['my body'], which, after all, is only derived from vulgar apprehensions."

The need to resist arguments from "vulgar apprehensions" holds more broadly: for such phrases as "my thoughts," "my dreams," "my spirit," even "my self," which is different from myself (= me, even though in another sense, I may not be myself these days). When John thinks about himself, he is thinking about John, but not when he is thinking about his self; he can hurt himself but not his self (whatever role these curious entities play in our mental world). There's a difference between saying that his actions are betraying his true (authentic, former) self and that he's betraying himself, and "thine own self" indicates a more essential characteristic than "thyself." Inquiry into manifold questions like these, while entirely legitimate and perhaps enlightening, is concerned with the "operations of the mind," our modes of cognition and thought, and should not be misinterpreted as holding of the "real objects that exist independently of our thought." The latter is the concern of the natural sciences, and I take it also to be the prime concern of the tradition reviewed here.

The operations of the mind doubtless accommodate the thesis that "I am not identical to my body," a core assumption of substance dualism, Stephen Yablo proposes.[60] He suggests further that "substance dualism . . . fallen strangely out of view," perhaps "because one no longer recognizes 'minds' as entities in their own right, or 'substances,'" though "*selves*— the things we refer to by use of 'I'—are surely substances, and it does little violence to the intention behind mind/body dualism to interpret it as a dualism of bodies and selves." In the tradition I am following here, it is *matter* that has lost its presumed status, and not "strangely." It is also by no means clear, as just noted, that by use of the first-person pronoun (as in "I pledge to devote my body and my soul"), or the name "John," we refer to *selves*. But truth or falsity aside, an argument would be needed to show that in using such words we refer (or even take ourselves to be referring) to real constituents of the world that exist independently of our modes of thought. An alternative, which seems to me more plausible, is that these topics belong not to natural science but rather to a branch of ethnoscience, a study of how people think about the world, a very different domain. For natural science, it seems hard to improve on Priestley's conclusion: that Locke's suggestion was fundamentally accurate and that properties "termed mental" reduce to "the organical structure of the brain"—though in ways that are not understood, no great surprise when we consider the history of even the core hard sciences, like chemistry.

As noted earlier, with the collapse of the traditional notion of body (etc.), there are basically two ways to reconstitute some problem that resembles the traditional mind-body problem: define *physical*, or set the problem up in other terms, such as those that Priestley anticipated.

Galen Strawson develops the first option in an important series of publications.[61] Unlike many others, he does give a definition of "physical," so that it is possible to formulate a physical-nonphysical problem. The physical is "any sort of existent [that is] spatio-temporally (or at least temporally) located." The physical includes "experiential events" (more generally mental events) and permits formulation of the question of how experiential phenomena can be physical phenomena—a "mind-body problem," in a post-Newtonian version. Following Eddington and Russell, and earlier antecedents, notably Priestley, Strawson concludes that "physical stuff has, in itself, 'a nature capable of manifesting itself as mental activity,' i.e., as experience or consciousness."

That much seems uncontroversial, given the definitions along with some straightforward facts. But Strawson intends to establish the much stronger thesis of *micropsychism* (which he identifies here with *panpsychism*): "at least some ultimates are intrinsically experience-involving." The crucial premise for that further conclusion, as Strawson makes explicit, is the No-Radical Emergence Thesis, already discussed, from which it follows that "experiential reality cannot possibly emerge from wholly and utterly non-experiential reality," a metaphysical issue, not an epistemic one. Strawson interprets Eddington's position to be *micropsychism*, citing his observation that it would be "rather silly to prefer to attach [thought] to something of a so-called 'concrete' nature inconsistent with thought, and then to wonder where the thought comes from," and that we have no knowledge "of the nature of atoms that renders it all incongruous that they should constitute a thinking object." This, however, appears to fall short of Strawson's micropsychism/panpsychism. Rather, Eddington seems to go no farther than Priestley's conception, writing that nothing in physics leads us to reject the conclusion that an "assemblage of atoms constituting a brain" can be "a thinking (conscious, experiencing) object." He does not, it seems, adopt the No-Radical Emergence Thesis that is required to carry the argument beyond to Strawson's conclusion. Russell too stops short of this critical step, and Priestley explicitly rejects it, regarding radical emergence as normal science. Textual interpretation aside, the issues seem fairly clearly drawn.

The second option is pursued by Daniel Stoljar, who has done some of the most careful work on physicalism and variants of the "mind-body problem." He does offer some answers to the question of what it means to say that something is *physical*—a question that, he notes, has not received a great deal of attention in the literature, though "without any understanding of what the physical is, we can have no serious understanding of what physicalism is."[62] The answers he offers are not too convincing, I think he would agree, but he argues that it does not matter much: "we have many concepts that we understand without knowing how to analyze," and "the concept of the physical is one of the central concepts of human thought." The latter comment is correct, but only with regard to the commonsense concept of the mechanical philosophy, long ago undermined. The former is correct, too, but it is not clear that we want to found a serious philosophical position on a concept that we think we understand intuitively but cannot analyze, particularly when a long history reveals that such commonsense understanding can often not withstand serious inquiry. But Stoljar's more fundamental reason for not being too concerned with characterizing the "physical" is different: the issues, he argues, should be shifted to epistemological terms, not seeking reduction to *the physical*, but taking physicalism to be only the "background metaphysical assumption against which the problems of philosophy of mind are posed and discussed." Thus "when properly understood, the problems that philosophers of mind are interested in are not with the framework [itself], and to that extent are not metaphysical."

Stoljar suggests that "the problem mainly at issue in contemporary philosophy is distinct *both* from the mind-body problem as that problem is traditionally understood *and* from the problem as it is, or might be, pursued in the sciences"; a qualification, I think, is that the traditional problem, at least from Descartes through Priestley (taking the latter's work to be the culmination of the post-Newtonian reaction to the traditional problem), can plausibly be construed as a problem within the sciences. The traditional questions "we may lump together under the heading 'metaphysics of mind,'" but contemporary philosophy Stoljar takes to be concerned with "epistemic principles" and, crucially, *the logical problem of experience*." It might be true that "the notion of the physical fails to meet minimal standards of clarity," he writes, but such matters "play only an illustrative or inessential role in the logical problem," which can be posed "even in the absence of . . . a reasonably definite conception of the physical."[63] The logical problem arises from the assumption that (1) there are experiential truths, while it seems plausible to believe both that (2) every such truth is entailed by (or supervenes on) some nonexperiential truth and that (3) not every experiential truth is entailed (or supervenes on) some nonexperiential truth. Adopting (1) and (2) (with a qualification to be considered), the crucial question is (3). As already discussed, following a tradition tracing back to Newton and Locke, Priestley sees no reason to accept thesis (3): our "very ignorance" of the properties of post-Newtonian *matter* cautions us not to take this step. In Russell's words (which Stoljar cites), experiential truths "are not known to have any intrinsic character which physical events cannot have, since we do not know of any intrinsic character which could be incompatible with the logical properties that physics assigns to physical events." From these perspectives, then, the logical problem does not arise.[64]

Stoljar's solution to the logical problem, the new "mind-body problem," is similar to the stance of Priestley and Russell, even if put somewhat differently. It is based on his "ignorance hypothesis, according to which we are ignorant of a type of experience-relevant nonexperiential truth," so that the "logical problem of experience" unravels on epistemic grounds.[65] He suggests elsewhere that "the radical view . . . that we are ignorant of the nature of the physical or non-experiential has the potential to completely transform philosophy of mind."[66] In Strawson's formulation, the (sensible) line of thought that was well understood up to a half century ago "disappeared almost completely from the philosophical mainstream [as] analytical philosophy acquired hyperdualist intuitions even as it proclaimed its monism. With a few honorable exceptions it out-Descartesed Descartes (or 'Descartes' [that is, the constructed version]) in its certainty that we know enough about the physical to know that the experiential cannot be physical."[67]

The qualification with regard to (2) is that we cannot so easily assume that there are nonexperiential truths; in fact the assumption may be "silly," as Eddington put it. Some physicists have reached such conclusions on quantum-theoretic grounds. John Wheeler argued that the "ultimates" may be just "bits of information," responses to queries posed by the investigator. According to H. P. Stapp, "The actual events of quantum theory are experienced increments in knowledge."[68] Russell's three grades of certainty suggest other reasons for skepticism. At least, some caution is necessary about the legitimacy even of the formulation of the "logical problem."

Stoljar invokes the ignorance hypothesis in criticizing C. D. Broad's conclusions about irreducibility of chemistry to physics, a close analog to the Knowledge Argument, he observes. He concludes that Broad was unaware "that chemical facts follow from physical facts," namely, the quantum-theoretic facts.[69] But putting the matter that way is somewhat misleading. What happened is that physics radically changed with the quantum-theoretic revolution, and with it the notion of "physical facts." A more appropriate formulation, I think, is to recognize that post-Newton, the concept "physical facts" means nothing more than what the best current scientific theory postulates, hence should be seen as a rhetorical device of clarification, adding no substantive content. The issue of physicalism cannot be so easily dispensed with. Like Marx's old mole, it keeps poking its nose out of the ground.

There are also lesser grades of mystery, worth keeping in mind. One of particular interest to humans is the evolution of their cognitive capacities. On this topic, evolutionary biologist Richard Lewontin has argued forcefully that we can learn very little, because evidence is inaccessible, at least in any terms understood by contemporary science.[70] For language, there are two fundamental questions in this regard: first, the evolution of the capacity to construct an infinite range of hierarchically structured expressions interpretable by our cognitive and sensorimotor systems; and second, the evolution of the atomic elements, roughly word-like, that enter into these computations. In both cases, the capacities appear to be specific to humans, perhaps even specific to language, apart from the natural laws they obey, which may have rather far-reaching consequences, recent work suggests. I think something can be said about the first of these questions, the evolution of the generative mechanisms. One conclusion that looks increasingly plausible is that externalization of language by means of the sensorimotor system is an ancillary process and also the locus of much of the variety and complexity of language. The evolution of atoms of computation, however, seems mired in mystery, whether we think of them as concepts or lexical items of language. In symbolic systems of other animals, symbols appear to be linked directly to mind-independent events. The symbols of human language are sharply different. Even in the simplest cases, there is no word–object relation, where objects are mind-independent entities. There is no reference relation, in the technical sense familiar from Frege and Peirce to contemporary externalists. Rather, it appears that we should adopt something like the approach of the seventeenth- and eighteenth-century cognitive revolution, and the conclusions of Shaftesbury and Hume that the "peculiar nature belonging to" the linguistic elements used to refer is not something external and mind-independent. Rather, their peculiar nature is a complex of perspectives involving Gestalt properties, cause-and-effect, "sympathy of parts" directed to a "common end," psychic continuity, and other such mental properties. In Hume's phrase, the "identity, which we ascribe" to vegetables, animal bodies, artifacts, or "the mind of man"—the array of individuating properties—is only a "fictitious one," established by our "cognoscitive powers," as they were termed by his seventeenth-century predecessors. That is no impediment to interaction, including the special case of communication, given largely shared cognoscitive powers. Rather, the semantic properties of words seem similar in this regard to their phonetic properties. No one is so deluded as to believe that there is a mind-independent object corresponding to the internal syllable [ba], some construction from motion of molecules perhaps, which is selected when I say [ba] and when you hear it. But interaction proceeds nevertheless, always a more-or-less rather than a yes-or-no affair.[71]

There is a lot to say about these topics, but I will not pursue them here, merely commenting that in this case too, there may be merit to Strawson's conclusion that "hyperdualist intuitions" should be abandoned along with the "certainty that we know enough about the physical to know that the experiential cannot be physical," and Stoljar's suggestion that "the radical view" might transform philosophy of mind and language, if taken seriously.

Returning finally to the core example of Cartesian science, human language, Gassendi's advice to seek a "chemical-like" understanding of its internal nature has been pursued with some success, but what concerned the Cartesians was something different: the creative use of language, what Humboldt later called "the infinite use of finite means," stressing *use*.[72]

There is interesting work on precepts for language use under particular conditions—notably intent to be informative, as in neo-Gricean pragmatics—but it is not at all clear how far this extends to the normal use of language, and in any event, it does not approach the Cartesian questions of creative use, which remains as much of a mystery now as it did centuries ago, and may turn out to be one of those ultimate secrets that ever will remain in obscurity, impenetrable to human intelligence.

NOTES

FOREWORD

1. For all references, see the chapters from which the quotations are taken. On the relation between language and thought, Chomsky, though he now thinks it to be even closer than he once did, does not think it is necessary to assert something as strong as "identity" between them, as Humboldt does. Descartes and Darwin, who also figure in Chomsky's discussion of the relation, did not go that far.

2. Although Chomsky mentions E-languages by way of contrast with I-languages, he doubts the coherence of the very idea and therefore whether they exist. In a number of his essays, he is critical of the most basic assumptions that philosophers make about their coherence, in giving accounts of them.

3. In making this point about study at a level of abstraction with a view to an eventual account in terms of the brain, Chomsky points out how the approach is no different in the scientific study of language than it is, for instance, in insect navigation. In other work, Chomsky cites some progress that might have been made in the inquiry into biological underpinnings, but also cites how there may also be some fundamentally wrong assumptions being made by brain scientists about what the object of study is. On this last point, see his reference to Charles Gallistel's work in chapter 2.

4. I owe this example to Carol Rovane. See Carol Rovane and Akeel Bilgrami, "Mind, Language, and the Limits of Inquiry," in *The Cambridge Companion to Chomsky*, ed. James McGilvray (Cambridge: Cambridge University Press, 2005), 181–203.

5. This should be qualified by pointing out that Chomsky, at the end of this chapter, actually discusses an argument in Peirce that appeals to biological considerations—in particular, evolutionary considerations based on natural selection (which he finds completely fallacious). This would suggest that Peirce was himself somewhat ambivalent about whether or not to see his overall methodological claim regarding admissible hypotheses and limits on them as owing to our biology.

6. And before Newton, motion was considered to be "the hard problem" by William Petty and others.

7. Chomsky was the first to stress this side of Smith many decades ago, a side of him that has been pursued in some detail much more recently in scholarship by Emma Rothschild and commentary by Amartya Sen.

8. One might add that there are issues on which the state can be justified because it may protect not just the marginalized and impoverished but *everyone* from their folly and doom, issues such as those of the environment, for instance, and more generally protect citizens from the cultural detritus and psychological desolation (issues of "alienation," in a word) that afflict capitalist societies.

1. WHAT IS LANGUAGE?

1. Charles Darwin, *The Descent of Man* (London: Murray, 1871), chap. 3.

2. Ian Tattersall, *Masters of the Planet: The Search for Our Human Origins* (New York: Palgrave Macmillan, 2012), xi.

3. The term is mine. See Noam Chomsky, *Knowledge of Language: Its Nature, Origin, and Use* (New York: Praeger, 1986). But I defined it almost vacuously, as any concept of language other than I-language.

4. A source of misunderstanding may be that in early work, "language" is sometimes defined in introductory expository passages in terms of weak generation, though the usage was quickly qualified, for reasons explained.

5. Ferdinand de Saussure, *Course in General Linguistics* (1916; repr., New York: Philosophical Library, 1959), 13–14; Leonard Bloomfield, "Philosophical Aspects of Language" (1942), in *A Leonard Bloomfield Anthology*, ed. Charles F. Hockett (Bloomington: Indiana University Press, 1970), 267–70; Bloomfield, *A Set of Postulates for the Science of Language* (In-

dianapolis: Bobbs-Merrill, 1926); Bloomfield, "A Set of Postulates for the Science of Language," *Language* 2, no. 3 (1926): 153–64; William Dwight Whitney, *The Life and Growth of Language: An Outline of Linguistic Science* (London: King, 1875); Edward Sapir, *Language: An Introduction to the Study of Speech* (New York: Harcourt, Brace, 1921), 8.

6. Martin Joos, comments in *Readings in Linguistics: The Development of Descriptive Linguistics in America Since 1925*, ed. Martin Joos (Washington, D.C.: American Council of Learned Societies, 1958).

7. Zellig Harris, *Methods in Structural Linguistics* (Chicago: University of Chicago Press, 1951).

8. A regression, I think, since it confuses the fundamentally different notions competence and performance—roughly, what we know and what we do—unlike Harris's system, which does not.

9. Dan Dediu and Stephen C. Levinson, "On the Antiquity of Language: The Reinterpretation of Neandertal Linguistic Capacities and Its Consequences," *Frontiers in Psychology* 4, no. 397 (2013): 1–17, doi:10.3389/fpsyg.2013.00397.

10. Galileo Galilei, *Dialogue Concerning the Two Chief World Systems* (1632), end of "The First Day."

11. For references and discussion, see Noam Chomsky, *Cartesian Linguistics: A Chapter in the History of Rationalist Thought*, 3rd ed., ed., with introduction, James McGilvray (Cambridge: Cambridge University Press, 2009).

12. Wilhelm von Humboldt, *On Language: On the Diversity of Human Language Construction and Its Influence on the Mental Development of the Human Species*, trans. Peter Heath (1836; New York: Cambridge University Press, 1988), 91.

13. Otto Jespersen, *The Philosophy of Grammar* (New York: Holt, 1924).

14. Mariacristina Musso et al., "Broca's Area and the Language Instinct," *Nature Neuroscience* 4 (2003): 774–81, doi:10.1038/nn1077.

15. Neil Smith, *Chomsky: Ideas and Ideals*, 2nd ed. (Cambridge: Cambridge University Press, 2004), 136. See also Neil Smith and Ianthi-Maria Tsimpli, *The Mind of a Savant: Language Learning and Modularity* (Cambridge: Blackwell, 1995).

16. Robert C. Berwick, Paul Pietroski, Beracah Yankama, and Noam Chomsky, "Poverty of the Stimulus Revisited," *Cognitive Science* 35, no. 7 (2011): 1207–42, doi:10.1111/j.1551–6709.2011.01189.x.

17. W. Tecumseh Fitch, "Speech Perception: A Language-Trained Chimpanzee Weighs In," *Current Biology* 21, no. 14 (2011): R543–46, doi:10.1016/j.cub.2011.06.035.

18. Charles Fernyhough, "The Voices Within: The Power of Talking to Yourself," *New Scientist*, June 3, 2013, 32–35.

19. William Uzgalis, "John Locke," in *The Stanford Encyclopedia of Philosophy* (Fall 2012 ed.), ed. Edward N. Zalta, http://plato.stanford.edu/archives/fall2012/entries/locke/.

20. Tue Trinh, "A Constraint on Copy Deletion," *Theoretical Linguistics* 35, nos. 2–3 (2009): 183–227. I also put aside here several topics that raise a variety of further questions, among them "covert operations" in which only the first-merged copy is externalized.

21. Patricia S. Churchland, foreword to W. V. O. Quine, *Word and Object* (1960; repr., Cambridge, Mass.: MIT Press, 2013), xiii.

22. Luigi Rizzi, *Issues in Italian Syntax* (Dordrecht: Foris, 1982).

2. WHAT CAN WE UNDERSTAND?

1. Owen Flanagan, *The Science of the Mind*, 2nd ed. (Cambridge, Mass.: MIT Press, 1991), 313. See also "New Mysterianism," Wikipedia, http://en.wikipedia.org/wiki/New_Mysterianism.

2. Noam Chomsky, "Problems and Mysteries in the Study of Human Language," in *Language in Focus: Foundations, Methods and Systems: Essays in Memory of Yehoshua Bar-Hillel*, ed. Asa Kasher (Boston: Reidel, 1976), 281–358. An extended version is in Chomsky, *Reflections on Language* (New York: Pantheon, 1975), chap. 4.

3. Noam Chomsky, *Language and Mind* (New York: Harcourt, Brace & World, 1968), 78–79.

4. Michael D. Gershon, *The Second Brain: The Scientific Basis of Gut Instinct and a Groundbreaking New Understanding of Nervous Disorders of the Stomach and Intestine* (New York: HarperCollins, 1998).

5. For more on this topic, and some of the other matters discussed later, see chapter 4.

6. Bertrand Russell, *The Analysis of Matter* (New York: Harcourt, Brace, 1927), chap. 37; C. I. Lewis, *Mind and the World-Order: Outline of a Theory of Knowledge* (New York: Scribner, 1929).

7. Galen Strawson, *The Evident Connexion: Hume on Personal Identity* (Oxford: Oxford University Press, 2011), 56.

8. Ibid., part 3.

9. John Locke, "Mr. Locke's Reply to the Bishop of Worcester's [Edward Stillingfleet] Answer to his Second Letter," in *The Works of John Locke in Nine Volumes*, 12th ed. (London: Rivington, 1824), 3:191, http://oll.liberty fund.org/titles/1724, discussed in Andrew Janiak, *Newton as Philosopher* (Cambridge: Cambridge University Press, 2008), 121.

10. Janiak, *Newton as Philosopher*, 9–10, 39.

11. On "Locke's suggestion" and its development through the eighteenth century, culminating in Priestley's important work, see John W. Yolton, *Thinking Matter: Materialism in Eighteenth-Century Britain* (Minneapolis: University of Minnesota Press, 1983); and some further elaboration in chapter 4.

12. Charles Darwin, Notebook C166, 1838, in *Charles Darwin's Notebooks, 1836–1844: Geology, Transmutation of Species, Metaphysical Enquiries*, ed. Paul H. Barrett et al. (Cambridge: Cambridge University Press, 1987), 291, http://darwin-online.org.uk/content/frameset?viewtype=image&itemID =CUL-DAR122.-&keywords=brain+the+of+secretion&pageseq=148.

13. Paul Churchland, "Betty Crocker's Theory," review of *The Rediscovery of the Mind*, by John R. Searle, *London Review of Books*, May 12, 1994, 13–14. Churchland associates Searle's views with Descartes's in ways that are not entirely clear, in part because of a misinterpretation of the mechanical philosophy and its fate. On Priestley and others, see Yolton, *Thinking Matter*; and chapter 4.

14. Vernon B. Mountcastle, "Brain Science at the Century's Ebb," in "The Brain," special issue, *Dædalus* 127, no. 2 (1998): 1.

15. Charles R. Gallistel and Adam Philip King, *Memory and the Computational Brain: Why Cognitive Science Will Transform Neuroscience* (Malden, Mass.: Wiley-Blackwell, 2009).

16. Thomas Nagel, "The Core of 'Mind and Cosmos,'" *New York Times*, August 18, 2013; Nagel, *Mind and Cosmos: Why the Materialist Neo-Darwinian*

Conception of Nature Is Almost Certainly False (New York: Oxford University Press, 2012).

17. David Hume, *The History of England* (1756), 6:chap. 71.

18. Udo Thiel, *The Early Modern Subject: Self-Consciousness and Personal Identity from Descartes to Hume* (Oxford: Oxford University Press, 2011).

19. Donald D. Hoffman, *Visual Intelligence: How We Create What We See* (New York: Norton, 1998), 159.

20. Richard Lewontin, "The Evolution of Cognition: Questions We Will Never Answer," in *An Invitation to Cognitive Science*, vol. 4, *Methods, Models, and Conceptual Issues*, ed. Don Scarborough and Saul Sternberg, 2nd ed. (Cambridge, Mass.: MIT Press, 1998), 108–32.

21. Marc Hauser et al., "The Mystery of Language Evolution," *Frontiers in Psychology* 5, no. 401 (2014): 1–12, doi:10.3389/fpsyg.2014.00401.

22. Laura-Ann Petitto, "How the Brain Begets Language," in *The Cambridge Companion to Chomsky*, ed. James McGilvray (Cambridge: Cambridge University Press, 2005), 86.

23. Peter Strawson, "On Referring," *Mind* 59, no. 235 (1950): 320–44; Julius Moravcsik, "*Aitia* as Generative Factor in Aristotle's Philosophy," *Dialogue* 14, no. 4 (1975): 622–36; Akeel Bilgrami, *Belief and Meaning: The Unity and Locality of Mental Content* (Oxford: Blackwell, 1992).

24. Aristotle, *Metaphysics*, book 8:3; *De Anima*, book 1:1.

25. Noam Chomsky, "Notes on Denotation and Denoting," in *From Grammar to Meaning: The Spontaneous Logicality of Language*, ed. Ivano Caponigro and Carlo Cecchetto (Cambridge: Cambridge University Press, 2013), 38–45, and sources cited there.

26. Cited in Ben Lazare Mijuskovic, *The Achilles of Rationalist Arguments* (The Hague: Nijhoff, 1974).

27. John Locke, *An Essay Concerning Human Understanding* (1689), book 2, chap. 27.

28. On women, see Linda K. Kerber, "Why Diamonds Really Are a Girl's Best Friend: Another American Narrative," *Dædalus* 141, no. 1 (2012): 89–100; and *Taylor v. Louisiana*, 419 U.S. 522 (1975). On African Americans, see Douglas Blackmon, *Slavery by Another Name: The Re-Enslavement of Black Americans from the Civil War to World War II* (New York: Doubleday, 2008); and Michelle L. Alexander, *The New Jim Crow: Mass Incarcera-*

tion in the Age of Colorblindness, rev. ed. (New York: New Press, 2012). On aliens, see *Rasul v. Myers*, Court of Appeals, District of Columbia Circuit, January 2008, April 2009. On corporations, see sources in Noam Chomsky, *Hopes and Prospects* (Chicago: Haymarket, 2010), 30–31; and David Ellerman, "Workplace Democracy and Human Development: The Example of the Postsocialist Transition Debate," *Journal of Speculative Philosophy* 24, no. 4 (2010): 333–53.

29. Dagfinn Føllesdal, "Indeterminacy and Mental States," in *Perspectives on Quine*, ed. Robert Barrett and Roger Gibson (Cambridge: Blackwell, 1990), 98–109.

30. Charles R. Gallistel, "Representations in Animal Cognition: An Introduction," *Cognition* 37, nos. 1–2 (1990): 1–22.

31. Daniel C. Dennett, "Sakes and Dints," *Times Literary Supplement*, March 2, 2012.

32. Noam Chomsky, "Derivation by Phase," in *Ken Hale: A Life in Language*, ed. Michael J. Kenstowicz (Cambridge, Mass.: MIT Press, 2001), 1–52.

33. Thiel, *Early Modern Subject*.

34. An inquiry that Colin McGinn has undertaken in several books and papers, among them *Basic Structures of Reality: Essays in Meta-Physics* (New York: Oxford University Press, 2011).

35. Susan Carey, *The Origin of Concepts* (Oxford: Oxford University Press, 2011).

36. For sources, see chapter 4.

37. David Hilbert, "Logic and the Knowledge of Nature" (1930), in *From Kant to Hilbert: A Source Book in the Foundations of Mathematics*, ed. William B. Ewald (New York: Oxford University Press, 2005), 2:1157–65. I am indebted to Richard Larson for this reference.

38. David Deutsch, *The Beginning of Infinity: Explanations That Transform the World* (New York: Viking, 2011); David Albert, "Explaining It All: How We Became the Center of the Universe," *New York Times*, August 12, 2011.

39. Chomsky, *Language and Mind*.

40. Juan Huarte de San Juan, *Examen de ingenios para las ciencias* (The examination of men's wits; 1575–1594). See Noam Chomsky, *Cartesian Linguistics: A Chapter in the History of Rationalist Thought*, 3rd ed., ed., with introduction, James McGilvray (Cambridge: Cambridge University Press,

2009); and Javier Virués Ortega, "Juan Huarte de San Juan in Cartesian and Modern Psycholinguistics: An Encounter with Noam Chomsky," *Psicothema* 17, no. 3 (2005): 436–40, http://www.psicothema.com/pdf/3125.pdf.

3. WHAT IS THE COMMON GOOD?

1. Adam Smith, *An Inquiry into the Nature and Causes of the Wealth of Nations*, ed. Edwin Cannan (1776; Chicago: University of Chicago Press, 1976), book 5, chap. 1, part 3, art. 2 (ii, 302–3).

2. Adam Smith, *The Theory of Moral Sentiments* (1759; New York: Penguin, 2009); "vile maxim": Smith, *Wealth of Nations*, book 3, chap. 4 (i, 437).

3. Rudolf Rocker, *Anarcho-Syndicalism: Theory and Practice* (London: Secker and Warburg, 1938).

4. Nathan Schneider, "Introduction: Anarcho-Curious? Or, Anarchist America," in *On Anarchism*, by Noam Chomsky (New York: New Press, 2013), xi.

5. United States Army, School of the Americas, May 1999, cited in Adam Isacson and Joy Olson, *Just the Facts: A Civilian's Guide to U.S. Defense and Security Assistance to Latin America and the Caribbean* (Washington, D.C.: Latin America Working Group, 1999).

6. John H. Coatsworth, "The Cold War in Central America, 1975–1991," in *The Cambridge History of the Cold War*, vol. 3, *Endings*, ed. Melvyn P. Leffler and Odd Arne Westad (Cambridge: Cambridge University Press, 2010), 221.

7. David Ellerman, *Property and Contract in Economics: The Case for Economic Democracy* (Cambridge: Blackwell, 1992).

8. Biorn Maybury-Lewis, *The Politics of the Possible: The Brazilian Rural Workers' Trade Union Movement, 1964–1985* (Philadelphia: Temple University Press, 1994).

9. Martin Gilens, *Affluence and Influence: Economic Inequality and Political Power in America* (Princeton, N.J.: Princeton University Press, 2012); Larry M. Bartels, *Unequal Democracy: The Political Economy of the New Gilded Age* (Princeton, N.J.: Princeton University Press, 2010).

10. Elizabeth Rosenthal, "Health Care's Road to Ruin," *New York Times*, December 21, 2013; Gardiner Harris, "In American Health Care, Drug Shortages Are Chronic," *New York Times*, October 31, 2004.

11. Kaiser Health Tracking Poll, April 2009. On polls, see Noam Chomsky, *Failed States: The Abuse of Power and the Assault on Democracy* (New York: Metropolitan Books / Holt, 2006), chap. 6. On constitutional right, see Robert H. Wiebe, *Self-Rule: A Cultural History of American Democracy* (Chicago: University of Chicago Press, 1995), 239.

12. Conor Gearty, *Liberty and Security* (Malden, Mass.: Polity, 2013).

13. Quotations from Robert B. Westbrook, *John Dewey and American Democracy* (Ithaca, N.Y.: Cornell University Press, 1991).

14. For more on Mill's and related views, see David Ellerman, "Workplace Democracy and Human Development: The Example of the Postsocialist Transition Debate," *Journal of Speculative Philosophy* 24, no. 4 (2010): 333–53.

15. Norman Ware, *The Industrial Worker, 1840–1860: The Reaction of the American Industrial Society to the Advance of the Industrial Revolution* (1924; repr., Chicago: Quadrangle Books, 1964).

16. See, among others, Lawrence Goodwyn, *The Populist Moment: A Short History of the Agrarian Revolt in America* (New York: Oxford University Press, 1978).

17. Jonathan Rose, *The Intellectual Life of the British Working Classes* (New Haven, Conn.: Yale University Press, 2002).

18. Walter Lippmann, *The Phantom Public*, in *The Essential Lippmann: A Political Philosophy for Liberal Democracy*, ed. Clinton Rossiter and James Lare (Cambridge, Mass.: Harvard University Press, 1982), 91–92; Edward Bernays, *Propaganda* (New York: Liveright, 1928); Harold Lasswell, "Propaganda," in *Encyclopedia of the Social Sciences*, ed. Edwin Seligman (New York: Macmillan, 1937); Michel J. Crozier, Samuel P. Huntington, and Joji Watanuki, *The Crisis of Democracy: Report on the Governability of Democracies to the Trilaterial Commission* (New York: New York University Press, 1975).

19. Jonathan Elliot, ed., *The Debates in the Several State Conventions on the Adoption of the Federal Constitution, 1787*, http://oll.libertyfund.org/

titles/1904. For further references to Madison and sources, see Noam Chomsky, "Consent Without Consent: Reflections on the Theory and Practice of Democracy," *Cleveland State Law Review* 44, no. 4 (1996): 415–37.

20. John Foster Dulles, telephone call to Allen Dulles, June 19, 1958, "Minutes of Telephone Conversations of John Foster Dulles and Christian Herter," Eisenhower Presidential Library, Museum, and Boyhood Home, Abilene, Kansas.

21. Lance Banning, *The Sacred Fire of Liberty: James Madison and the Founding of the Federal Republic* (Ithaca, N.Y.: Cornell University Press, 1995), 245, citing Gordon S. Wood, *The Creation of the American Republic, 1776–1787* (Chapel Hill: University of North Carolina Press, 1969).

22. Banning, *Sacred Fire of Liberty*, 333.

23. Christopher Hill, *The World Turned Upside Down: Radical Ideas During the English Revolution* (New York: Penguin, 1975), 60.

24. Quoted in Charles Sellers, *The Market Revolution: Jacksonian America, 1815–1846* (New York: Oxford University Press, 1991), 269–70.

4. THE MYSTERIES OF NATURE

1. David Hume, *The History of England* (1756), 6:chap. 71; John Locke, *An Essay Concerning Human Understanding* (1689), book 4, chap. 3. Locke's reasons, of course, were not Hume's but relied on the boundaries of "the simple ideas we receive from sensation and reflection," which prevent us from comprehending the nature of body or mind (spirit).

2. Renée Baillargeon, "Innate Ideas Revisited: For a Principle of Persistence in Infants' Physical Reasoning," *Perspectives on Psychological Science* 3 (2008): 2–13.

3. I. Bernard Cohen, *Revolution in Science* (Cambridge, Mass.: Harvard University Press, 1985), 155.

4. Ernan McMullin, *Newton on Matter and Activity* (Notre Dame, Ind.: Notre Dame University Press, 1978), 52ff. McMullin concludes that because of Newton's vacillation in use of the terms "mechanical," "spirit," and others, it is "misleading . . . to take Newton to be an exponent of the 'mechanical philosophy'" (73).

5. Locke, *Essay Concerning Human Understanding*; and correspondence with Edward Stillingfleet, cited in Ben Lazare Mijuskovic, *The Achilles of Rationalist Arguments* (The Hague: Nijhoff, 1974), 73. On the development of "Locke's suggestion" through the eighteenth century, culminating in Joseph Priestley's work (discussed later), see John Yolton, *Thinking Matter: Materialism in Eighteenth-Century Britain* (Minneapolis: University of Minnesota Press, 1983).

6. Pierre-Jean-George Cabanis, *On the Relations Between the Physical and Moral Aspects of Man*, vol. 1 (1802; Baltimore: Johns Hopkins University Press, 1981).

7. Quoted in V. S. Ramachandran and Sandra Blakeslee, *Phantoms in the Brain: Probing the Mysteries of the Human Mind* (New York: Morrow, 1998), 227.

8. Isaac Newton, *Principia*, General Scholium (1713).

9. E. J. Dijksterhuis, *The Mechanization of the World Picture: Pythagoras to Newton*, trans. C. Dikshoorn (Oxford: Clarendon Press, 1961; repr., Princeton, N.J.: Princeton University Press, 1986), 479–80.

10. Ibid., 488; Isaac Newton to Richard Bentley, 1693, in *Newton: Philosophical Writings*, ed. Andrew Janiak (Cambridge: Cambridge University Press, 2004), 102–3.

11. For more detailed analysis, see McMullin, *Newton on Matter and Activity*, chap. 3.

12. Thomas Nagel, "Searle: Why We Are Not Computers," in *Other Minds: Critical Essays, 1969–1994* (New York: Oxford University Press, 1995), 106.

13. For varying perspectives on the "explanatory gap," see Galen Strawson et al., *Consciousness and Its Place in Nature: Does Physicalism Entail Panpsychism?*, ed. Anthony Freeman (Charlottesville, Va.: Imprint Academic, 2006).

14. Thomas Kuhn, *The Copernican Revolution: Planetary Astronomy in the Development of Western Thought* (New York: Random House, 1957), 259; Heinrich Hertz, quoted in McMullin, *Newton on Matter and Activity*, 124.

15. Dijksterhuis, *Mechanization of the World Picture*, 489.

16. Richard H. Popkin, *The History of Scepticism from Erasmus to Spinoza* (Berkeley: University of California Press, 1979), 139–40, 213.

17. Bertrand Russell, *Analysis of Matter* (New York: Harcourt, Brace, 1927; repr., New York: Dover, 1954), 18–19, 162.

18. Paul Dirac, *Principles of Quantum Mechanics* (Oxford: Clarendon Press, 1930), 10. I am indebted to John Frampton for this reference.

19. Peter Machamer, "Introduction" and "Galileo's Machines, His Mathematics, and His Experiments," in *The Cambridge Companion to Galileo*, ed. Peter Machamer (Cambridge: Cambridge University Press, 1998), 17, 69.

20. Cited in Pietro Redondi, "From Galileo to Augustine," in ibid., 175–210.

21. Daniel Stoljar, *Ignorance and Imagination: The Epistemic Origin of the Problem of Consciousness* (Oxford: Oxford University Press, 2006). Recall that Newton hoped that there might be a scientific (that is, mechanical) solution to the problems of matter and motion.

22. On these topics, see Noam Chomsky, *Cartesian Linguistics: A Chapter in the History of Rationalist Thought*, 3rd ed., ed., with introduction, James McGilvray (Cambridge: Cambridge University Press, 2009); and Chomsky, *Language and Mind* (New York: Harcourt, Brace & World, 1968), chap. 1. Note that the concerns go far beyond indeterminacy of free action, as is particularly evident in the experimental programs by Géraud de Cordemoy and others on "other minds" (see *Cartesian Linguistics*).

23. René Descartes to Queen Christina of Sweden, 1647, in *Principia Philosophiæ*, vol. 8 of *Oeuvres de Descartes*, ed. Charles Adam and Paul Tannery (Paris: Cerf, 1905). For discussion, see Tad Schmaltz, *Malebranche's Theory of the Soul: A Cartesian Interpretation* (New York: Oxford University Press, 1996), 204ff.

24. Noam Chomsky, "Turing on the 'Imitation Game,'" in *The Turing Test: Verbal Behavior as the Hallmark of Intelligence*, ed. Stuart Schieber (Cambridge, Mass.: MIT Press, 2004), 317–21.

25. Desmond Clarke, *Descartes's Theory of Mind* (Oxford: Clarendon Press, 2003), 12. See also Rene Descartes to Marin Mersenne, 1641, on the goal of the *Meditations*, cited in Margaret Wilson, *Descartes* (Boston: Routledge and Kegan Paul, 1978), 2.

26. Clarke, *Descartes's Theory of Mind*, 258.

27. Nancy Kanwisher and Paul Downing, "Separating the Wheat from the Chaff," *Science*, October 2, 1998, 57–58; Newton, General Scholium.

28. Eric R. Kandel and Larry R. Squire, "Neuroscience," *Science*, November 10, 2000, 1113–20.

29. Charles R. Gallistel, "Neurons and Memory," in *Conversations in the Cognitive Neurosciences*, ed. Michael S. Gazzaniga (Cambridge, Mass.: MIT Press, 1997), 71–89; Gallistel, "Symbolic Processes in the Insect Brain," in *An Invitation to Cognitive Science*, vol. 4, *Methods, Models, and Conceptual Issues*, ed. Don Scarborough and Saul Sternberg, 2nd ed. (Cambridge, Mass.: MIT Press, 1998), 1–51.

30. Semir Zeki, "Art and the Brain," *Daedalus* 127, no. 2 (1998): 71–104.

31. Nagel, "Searle," 106. For some cautionary notes on "sharp logical separation between the nervous system and the rest of the organism," see Charles Rockland, "The Nematode as a Model Complex System" (working paper [LIDS-WP-1865], Laboratory for Information and Decisions Systems, MIT, April 14, 1989), 30.

32. John Henry, "Occult Qualities and the Experimental Philosophy: Active Principles in Pre-Newtonian Matter Theory," *History of Science* 24 (1986): 335–81; Alan Kors, "The Atheism of D'Holbach and Naigeon," in *Atheism from the Reformation to the Enlightenment*, ed. Michael Hunger and David Wootton (Oxford: Clarendon Press, 1992), 273–300; Locke, *Essay Concerning Human Understanding*; Yolton, *Thinking Matter*, 199. For Voltaire and Kant, see McMullin, *Newton on Matter and Activity*, 113, 122–23 (from Kant, *Metaphysical Foundations of Natural Science* [1786]); Michael Friedman, "Kant and Newton: Why Gravity Is Essential to Matter," in *Philosophical Perspectives on Newtonian Science*, ed. Phillip Bricker and R. I. G. Hughes (Cambridge, Mass.: MIT Press, 1990), 185–202; and Howard Stein, "On Locke, 'the Great Huygenius, and the Incomparable Mr. Newton,'" in ibid., 17–48. Friedman argues that there is no contradiction between Newton and Kant because they do not mean the same thing by "essential," Kant having discarded Newton's metaphysics and making an epistemological point within his "Copernican revolution in metaphysics."

33. Friedrich Lange, *Geschichte des Materialismus und Kritik seiner Bedeutung in der Gegenwart* (1865), 3rd expanded ed. translated as *The History of Materialism and Criticism of Its Present Importance* (London: Kegan Paul, Trench, Trubner, 1925).

34. Alexandre Koyré, *From the Closed World to the Infinite Universe* (Baltimore: Johns Hopkins University Press, 1958), 210.

35. George V. Coyne, "The Scientific Venture and Materialism: False Premises," in *Space or Spaces as Paradigms of Mental Categories* (Milan: Fondazione Carlo Erba, 2000), 7–19.

36. Russell, *Analysis of Matter*, chap. 37. Russell did not work out how percepts in their cognitive aspect were assimilated into the "causal skeleton of the world," leaving him open to a counterargument by mathematician Max Newman (Russell to Newman, April 24, 1928, in *The Autobiography of Bertrand Russell*, vol. 2, *1914–1944* [Boston: Little Brown, 1967]).

37. Democritus, quoted in Erwin Schrödinger, *Nature and the Greeks* (Cambridge: Cambridge University Press, 1954), 89. I am indebted to Jean Bricmont for this reference.

38. Daniel Stoljar and Yujin Nagasawa, "Introduction," in *There's Something About Mary: Essays on Phenomenal Consciousness and Frank Jackson's Knowledge Argument*, ed. Peter Ludlow, Yujin Nagasawa, and Daniel Stoljar (Cambridge, Mass.: MIT Press, 2004), 1–36.

39. On Hume, see John Mikhail, "Rawls' Linguistic Analogy: A Study of the 'Generative Grammar' Model of Moral Theory Described by John Rawls in *A Theory of Justice*" (Ph.D. diss., Cornell University, 2000); Mikhail, *Elements of Moral Cognition: Rawls' Linguistic Analogy and the Cognitive Science of Moral and Legal Judgment* (Cambridge: Cambridge University Press, 2011); and Mikhail, "Universal Moral Grammar: Theory, Evidence, and the Future," *Trends in Cognitive Sciences* 11, no. 4 (2007): 143–52. On the irrelevance (and as it is formulated, even incoherence) of the doctrine of "accessibility to consciousness," see Noam Chomsky, *Reflections on Language* (New York: Pantheon, 1975); Chomsky, *Rules and Representations* (New York: Columbia University Press, 1980); and Chomsky, *New Horizons in the Study of Language and Mind* (Cambridge: Cambridge University Press, 2000). On the rules of visual perception, inaccessible to consciousness in the interesting cases, see Donald D. Hoffman, *Visual Intelligence: How We Create What We See* (New York: Norton, 1998).

40. Frank Jackson, "What Mary Didn't Know" and "Postscript," in *There's Something About Mary*, ed. Ludlow, Nagasawa, and Stoljar, xv–xix, 410–42.

41. Charles S. Peirce, "The Logic of Abduction," in *Essays in the Philosophy of Science*, ed. V. Tomas (New York: Liberal Arts Press, 1957). For discussion of Peirce's proposals, and fallacies invoking natural selection that led him to the ungrounded (and implausible) belief that our "guessing instinct" leads us to true theories, see Chomsky, *Language and Mind*, 90ff.

42. Quoted in Wilson, *Descartes*, 95.

43. David Hume, *An Inquiry Concerning Human Understanding* (1772), vol. 2.1. On dubious modern efforts to formulate what had been a reasonably clear project before the separation of philosophy from science, see Chomsky, *New Horizons in the Study of Language and Mind*, 79–80, 144–45, and generally chaps. 5 and 6 (reprinted from *Mind* 104 [1995]: 1–61).

44. On Joseph Black, see Robert E. Schofield, *Mechanism and Materialism: British Natural Philosophy in an Age of Reason* (Princeton, N.J.: Princeton University Press, 1970), 226; William Brock, *The Norton History of Chemistry* (New York: Norton, 1993), 271; and Arnold Thackray, *Atoms and Powers* (Cambridge, Mass.: Harvard University Press, 1970), 37–38, 276–77.

45. Brock, *Norton History of Chemistry*. For sources and further discussion, see Chomsky, *New Horizons in the Study of Language and Mind*; Noam Chomsky, *Knowledge of Language: Its Nature, Origins, and Use* (New York: Praeger, 1986), 251–52; and David Lindley, *Boltzmann's Atom: The Great Debate That Launched a Revolution in Physics* (New York: Free Press, 2001). Some argue that even if quantum-theoretic unification succeeds, "in some sense the program of reduction of chemistry to [the new] physics fails," in part because of "practical issues of intractability" (Maureen Christie and John Christie, "'Laws' and 'Theories' in Chemistry Do Not Obey the Rules," in *Of Minds and Molecules: New Philosophical Perspectives on Chemistry*, ed. Nalin Bhushan and Stuart Rosenfield [Oxford: Oxford University Press, 2000], 34–50).

46. Russell, *Analysis of Matter*, 388.

47. See note 39. Sometimes misunderstanding and distortion reach the level of the surreal. For some startling examples, see Noam Chomsky, "Symposium on Margaret Boden, Mind as Machine: A History of Cognitive Science, Oxford, 2006," *Artificial Intelligence* 171 (2007): 1094–1103. On "the

rigidity rule and [Shimon] Ullman's theorem," see Hoffman, *Visual Intelligence*, 159. Needless to say, the rule is inaccessible to consciousness.

48. Vernon B. Mountcastle, "Brain Science at the Century's Ebb," in "The Brain," special issue, *Dædalus* 127, no. 2 (1998): 1. For sources, see Chomsky, *New Horizons in the Study of Language and Mind*, chap. 5.

49. Joseph Priestley, "Materialism," from *Disquisitions Relating to Matter and Spirit* (1777), in *Priestley's Writings on Philosophy, Science, and Politics*, ed. John Passmore (New York: Collier-Macmillan, 1965).

50. Similar ideas appear pre-Newton, particularly in the *Objections to the Meditations*, where critics ask how Descartes can know, "without divine revelation . . . that God has not implanted in certain bodies a power or property enabling them to doubt, think, etc." (Catherine Wilson, "Commentary on Galen Strawson," in Strawson et al., *Consciousness and Its Place in Nature*, 178).

51. Priestley, "Materialism." For later discussion, see Yolton, *Thinking Matter*, 113. Julien Offrey de La Mettrie had drawn similar conclusions a generation earlier but in a different framework, and without addressing the Cartesian arguments to which he was attempting to respond. The same is true of Gilbert Ryle and other modern attempts. For some discussion, see Chomsky, *Cartesian Linguistics*.

52. For discussion and illustrations, see Chomsky, *New Horizons in the Study of Language and Mind*. For "hyperdualism," see Galen Strawson, "Realistic Monism: Why Physicalism Entails Panpsychism," in Strawson et al., *Consciousness and Its Place in Nature*, 3–31.

53. Thackray, *Atoms and Powers*, 190. Priestley's reasons for welcoming "this extreme development of the Newtonian position" were primarily theological, Thackray concludes.

54. Yolton, *Thinking Matter*, 114.

55. Ibid., 125. For discussion, see chaps. 5 and 6. Yolton writes that "there was no British La Mettrie," but that exaggerates La Mettrie's contribution, I believe. See note 51.

56. Nagel, "O'Shaughnessy: The Will," in *Other Minds*, 94.

57. Strawson, "Realistic Monism" and "Panpsychism? Reply to Commentators with a Celebration of Descartes," in Strawson et al., *Consciousness*

and Its Place in Nature, 3–31, 184–280. Printers errors corrected (Strawson, pers. comm.). For further discussion, see the essays in this volume.

58. Strawson, "Realistic Monism," "Panpsychism," and commentary.

59. Noam Chomsky, *Aspects of the Theory of Syntax* (Cambridge, Mass.: MIT Press, 1965), 199–200; for much more extensive discussion, see Chomsky, *Cartesian Linguistics*. On the accuracy of interpretations of the empiricist theory of ideas by Reid and others, see John Yolton, *Perceptual Acquaintance from Descartes to Reid* (Minneapolis: University of Minnesota Press, 1984), chap. 5.

60. Stephen Yablo, "The Real Distinction Between Mind and Body," *Canadian Journal of Philosophy*, suppl. 16 (1990): 149–201.

61. Quotations from Strawson, "Realistic Monism" and "Panpsychism."

62. Quotations in this paragraph from Daniel Stoljar, "Physicalism," in *The Stanford Encyclopedia of Philosophy* (Spring 2001 ed.), ed. Edward N. Zalta, http://plato.stanford.edu/archives/spr2001/entries/physicalism/.

63. Stoljar, *Ignorance and Imagination*, 56, 58.

64. Ibid., 17ff, 56–57, 104. Stoljar understands the "traditional problem" to be derived from the *Meditations* (45), hence not a problem of the sciences. But though a conventional reading, it is questionable, for reasons already discussed.

65. Ibid., chap. 4.

66. Daniel Stoljar, "Comments on Galen Strawson," in Strawson et al., *Consciousness and Its Place in Nature*, 170–76.

67. Strawson, "Realistic Monism," 11n.21.

68. John A. Wheeler, *At Home in the Universe* (New York: American Institute of Physics, 1994); H. P. Stapp, "Commentary on Strawson's Target Article," in Strawson et al., *Consciousness and Its Place in Nature*, 163–69.

69. Stoljar, *Ignorance and Imagination*, 139.

70. Richard C. Lewontin, "The Evolution of Cognition: Questions We Will Never Answer," in *Methods, Models, and Conceptual Issues*, ed. Scarborough and Sternberg, 107–32.

71. Chomsky, *Cartesian Linguistics*, 94ff. On Cartesian and neo-Platonist conceptions of the role of "cognoscitive powers," see James McGilvray, "Introduction to the Third Edition," in Chomsky, *Cartesian Linguistics*,

1–52. For review and sources on referring, see Chomsky, *New Horizons in the Study of Language and Mind*; on Shaftesbury, Hume, and forerunners, see Mijuskovic, *Achilles of Rationalist Arguments*.

72. On misunderstandings about this matter, see Noam Chomsky, "A Note on the Creative Aspect of Language Use," *Philosophical Review* 41, no. 3 (1982): 423–34.

Brock, William, 108
Brown, Roger, 42

capitalism: and change from price to wage, 73; Dewey on, 70–71; hindering of human development by, xxi; history of U.S. activism against ravages of, 72–75; necessity of state as protector of oppressed in, xxiii, 67; wrecking of classical liberalism by, 62
Carter administration, and U.S. plutocracy, 76
Cartesian dualism, 82–83; as common sense, 82–83; and creative character of language, 6–7, 93–94, 127; delay in supplanting of, by Newtonian physics, 88; end of, Priestley on, 113–14; and explanatory gap in explaining mental phenomenon, 94; and language as defining feature of humans, 93–94; modern forms of, 30; Newton's adherence to, xvi, 33–34, 83, 85, 86, 98–99; Newton's destruction of, xvi–xvii, 30, 33–34, 35, 52, 85, 111–12, 113–14. *See also* mechanical philosophy; mind-body problem
Catholicism: and Christian anarchism, 64; and liberation theology, 65–66
Catholic Workers Movement, 64
causative link to external objects: in animal signals, xviii–xix, 41–42,

126; lack of, in human language, xix, 7, 42–43
chemistry, unification of with physics: and abandonment of erroneous conception of physical laws, 36, 109, 124–25, 143n45; and ignorance hypothesis, 124; parallels of, with research in science of mind, 36, 109–11, 114, 120; pragmatic pursuit of, 106–9
Christian anarchism, 64
Churchland, Patricia, 21
Churchland, Paul, 35, 133n13
civil personality, of women and servants, 46
civil rights activism, and libertarian socialism, 63
Clarke, Desmond, 93–94
coercion, unjustified, dismantling of: as anarchist principle, xxiii, 61, 63–64, 66; Dewey on, 70–71
cognition: lack of accessible evidence on evolution of, xix, 39–40, 125; lack of evolution in, 40; scope of, as product of cognitive limits, 56–57, 59, 105. *See also* limits on human cognition
cognitive revolution, 126
cognitive science, tentative nature of progress in, vii
Cohen, I. Bernard, 83
Cole, G. D. H., 72
common good: as concept universally supported and everywhere violated, xxii, 60; definition of, 60;

individuality, and thingness as issue, 51–52

innate cognoscitive powers, and language acquisition, 47

insects, computational capacity of, 96

intelligibility: necessity of suspending concerns about, in scientific inquiry, 109, 116, 117; of Newtonian action at a distance, suspension of concerns about, xvii, 34, 98–99, 108; and radical emergence, as issue, 115, 116. *See also* pragmatic approach to inquiry

Invitation to Cognitive Science, An, 39–40

islands, 22–23

Jackson, Frank, 101, 102

Jacobi, Carl Gustav Jacob, 54–55

Janiak, Andrew, 34, 52

Jefferson, Thomas, 79–80

Jespersen, Otto, 8, 9

Johnson, Samuel, 31

Joos, Martin, 5–6

justice, as concept universally supported and everywhere violated, 60

Kandel, Eric, 95

Kant, Immanuel, xx, 46, 97, 141n32

Kanwisher, Nancy, 95

Katz, Jerrold, xi

Kekulé, August, 108

Kerry, John, 69

knowledge argument: and ignorance hypothesis, 124; vs. knowledge intuition, 101–2

knowledge intuition, vs. knowledge argument, 101–2

Korsch, Karl, 63

Koyré, Alexandre, 99

Kripke, Saul, 50

Kropotkin, Peter, 67

Kuhn, Thomas, 87–88

La Mettrie, Julien Offrey de, 144n51

Lange, Friedrich, 98–99

language: vs. animal signs, xviii–xix, 41–43, 48, 126; behaviorist accounts of, xii; as biological endowment, xi, xiv, 15, 20; common usage, theory of mind and, 117–19; communication as secondary to thought in, xi, xviii, 14–15, 16, 24, 125; facility of semantic interpretation vs. communication, 18–19, 22–23; as I-language, 4; as instrument of thought, 13–16, 23; as internal to individual subject, ix; lack of referential semantics in, 48; as mystery, 8, 92; pragmatic approach to study of, 109–11; pragmatics in, 48; syntax in, 48; and thought, relation between, 129n1; as unique to humans, xii, 59, 125; variety in, accounting for, 40–41, 125. *See also* acquisition of language; atomic elements of computation; communication;

of, 113–14; new biology on, 36, 110–11; parallel with apparent absurdity of action at a distance, 86–87; Priestley on, 35, 113–17, 120, 121, 123; Russell on, 120, 121; Stoljar on, 121–24; Strawson on, 120–21

PRAGMATIC APPROACH TO STUDY OF, 86, 87, 89, 109–11; and hope of eventual unity with neuro-science, 36, 105–6, 109–11, 127; parallels of, with early New-tonian investigations, 86–87, 89; and possibility of incorrect reduction base, 89; Priestley on, 117

mind-body problem: epistemologi-cal argument for, 6–7, 93–94, 127; evaporation of, after Newton, 104; and ignorance hypothesis, 91–92, 123–24, 127; and limits on human cognition, xvi–xvii; Russell on, 100–103. *See also* Cartesian dualism

RECONSTITUTION OF, 111–12; and "physical," redefinition of, 103, 120–21; and Priestley, 114–15; reinterpretation of, as body-self dualism, 119–20; Stoljar on, 121–24; Strawson on, 120–21. *See also* mind: as emergent property of brain

Minimal Computation principle: as basic principle of language, 11; and communication, 19, 24;

displacement as consequence of, xiii, 17–20; and islands, 22–23; and Merge operation, 16–17; minimal distance principle as subset of, 11; neuroscientific evidence for, 11–12; as part of UG, 20; and passivization, 22; and strong minimalist thesis, 24–25; as subset of general property of organic world, 11

minimal distance principle: in mental computation, ix–x, 10–12, 13, 17; as subset of Minimal Com-putation principle, 11

minimalist program, 24–25

mitigated skepticism, as method, 89, 105, 109. *See also* pragmatic approach to inquiry

MMM Thesis, 47–48

model-theoretic semantics, lack of in natural language, 48

Moore, G. E., 31

Moral Sentiments (Smith), 62

Moravcsik, Julius, 43

motion, as hard problem of early modern science, 32, 96–99. *See also* action at a distance, apparent absurdity of

Mountcastle, Vernon, 35–36, 111

mysterianism: acceptance of, by philosophers, 31–33, 37, 52–53, 54; and acceptance of mysteries-for-humans in scientific inquiry, xx, 32–34, 53–54, 88–90, 104; definition of, 27; denial of, by

Newtonian physics, delay of in supplanting Cartesian physics, 88
New York Times, 68, 69
NIM project, 42–43
nonexperiential truths: existence of, as issue, 124; supervenience of experiential truth on, as issue, 123–24
No-Radical Emergence Thesis (Strawson), 115–16, 121
noun phrases, and object status, 49, 118
null subject languages, 23

Obama, Barack, and Affordable Care Act, 69
Objections (Gassendi), 106
Objections to the Meditations (Descartes), 144n50
objects: mind-independent, troubled status of concept, 48–52; noun phrases and object status, 49, 118. *See also* referential properties
On Liberty (Mill), 60–61
Opticks (Newton), 83, 107
origin of language: animal signals as unlikely source of, xviii–xix, 48; and appearance of Merge, xiii; vs. communication, 40; Darwin on, 2–3; focus on communication, as misguided, 14–15, 40; gradual evolution model, unlikelihood of, xviii–xix, 48; Jespersen on, 8; lack of detectable evidence on, 40; Lewontin on, xix, 39–40, 52; as

mystery-for-humans, xix, 39–40, 52, 59; origin of atomic elements, as issue, 125–26; origin of infinite range of interpretable hierarchical expressions, as issue, 125; and phenotype, necessity of defining, xix, 6, 40, 41, 59; requirements for credible account of, 40–41; and SMT hypothesis, 25; as sudden, recent leap, xiii, 3, 25, 40; Tattersall on, 3, 25
other minds, as issue, and creative use of language, 93

Pannekoek, Anton, 63
panpsychism: Priestley's rejection of, 116, 117; and Strawson, 115–16, 120–21
parliamentary tradition: as instrument of class rule, 68; in seventeenth-century England, xxii
passivization, and communication vs. semantic interpretation, 22
Pauling, Linus, 109
Peirce, Charles Sanders: on abduction, xv, 27–28, 55–56; on limits on human cognition, xix, 28, 53, 105; and mysteries as roadblocks to inquiry, xx; on sign-object reference, 126
people, as guardians of public interest, 79–80
percepts as physical events, Russell on, 100–101, 102
Perrin, Jean Baptise, 23

person, as complex concept, 45–46

Peterloo massacre, 73

Petitto, Laura-Ann, 42–43

Petty, Sir William, 96–97

philosophy, contemporary: denial of mysteries by, xix; Stoljar on central problem of, 122–23; Strawson on hyperdualist intuitions of, 124, 127

philosophy, naturalization of in Hume, 106

philosophy of mind: and limits on human cognition, xvi–xvii; and mind-body problem, reengagement with, 111–12; questionable foundational assumptions of, 36; Stoljar on epistemological terms of, 122–23

phonetics, limited success of, 44

physicalism, Jackson on limitations of, 102

physics: and human perception, necessity of continuity between, 100, 102; Newtonian, delay of in supplanting Cartesian physics, 88; Russell on limits of, 100–103. *See also* chemistry, unification of with physics

Plutarch, and Ship of Theseus paradox, 50

Poincaré, Henri, 108

Politics (Aristotle), 79

Popkin, Richard, 89–90

positivists, on collapse of mechanical philosophy, 88

pragmatic approach to inquiry, 53–54; eventual adoption of, as scientific routine, 90; and fundamental unintelligibility of world, 90–91; in language, and hope of eventual unity with, 127; and mysterianism, xx, 32–34, 53–54, 88–90, 104; and Newton, xx, 53, 88–89, 99; and Priestley, 114; Russell on, 90; in study of mind and language, 36, 109–11; tradition of, before Newton, 89–90

IN CHEMISTRY: and abandonment of erroneous conception of physical laws, 109; and eventual unity with physics, 36, 106–9, 124–25, 143n45

FOR MENTAL PHENOMENA, 86, 87, 89, 109–11; and hope of eventual unity with neuroscience, 36, 105–6, 109–11, 127; parallels of, with early Newtonian investigations, 86–87, 89; and possibility of incorrect reduction base, 89; Priestley on, 117

pragmatics, neo-Gricean, 127

Priestley, Joseph: and collapse of mechanical philosophy, 111–12; and humans as one substance, 114; on limits on human cognition, xvi–xvii, xix; on Locke, 111, 113, 120; and matter-spirit dualism, end of, 113–14; on mind, as conscious assembly of unconscious parts, 117; on mind, as emergent property of brain, 35, 111–17, 120, 121, 123; and mind-body problem, reconstitution of, 114–15; on operations of mind vs. its products, 118, 119; and pragmatic method, 114; on self, as concept, 117; on study of mind, 117–19; on thought as physical process, 35, 114–15

Principia (Newton), 83

private property, protection of: Aristotle on, 79; as goal of U.S. system, 76–78

problems, vs. mysteries, xv, 27–29; effort to sharpen boundary between, 53

progressives, mainstream, on democracy, 75–76, 80

property. *See* private property, protection of

quantum physics: and abandonment of erroneous conceptions, unity of chemistry and physics through, 36, 106–9, 124–25, 143n45; and fundamental unintelligibility of world, 90; and nonexperiential truths, 124

Quine, W. V. O., xvii, 21, 38, 42, 47–49, 102

radical emergence, 115

Reagan, Ronald W., 46, 65

realist metaphysics, and acceptance of mysteries, xix–xx

red bureaucracy, xxi, 68

referentialist doctrine, 42, 44–45, 50

referential properties: as contextual, xviii, 43–44; lack of, in atomic elements of computation, xviii, 43–46, 126; lack of, in natural language, 48

Regulae ad directionem ingenii (Descartes), 92

Reid, Thomas, 118

Remerge, as nonexistent operation, 17–18

rigidity rule, Hoffman on, 38

Rizzi, Luigi, 23

Rocker, Rudolph, xxi, 62–63, 64, 66, 70

Rose, Jonathan, 75

rule-following, Quine on, 38

Russell, Bertrand: on certainty, three grades of, 100, 124; on chemical laws vs. physical laws, 36; on fundamental unintelligibility of world, 90, 100; on limits on human cognition, xix, 31, 32, 53, 104–5; on matter, unknowability of intrinsic character of, 100; on matter-spirit dualism, end of, 113–14; on mind as emergent property of brain, 120, 121, 123; neutral monism of, 99–100; on percepts as physical events, 100–101, 102, 142n36; on physics, limits of, 100–103; on physics and human perception, necessity of continuity between, 100–102; and pragmatic approach to

sign language, structural similarity
  of to spoken language, x, 13, 14
simplicity principle of scientific
  method, and computational
  procedure, xii–xiii, 16–17
slavery, and personhood, 46
Smith, Adam, xx–xxi, xxiii, 61–62, 71
Smith, Neil, 11–12
SMT. *See* strong minimalist thesis
socialism, as term, 62–63
soul, nature of, and identity as construct of imagination, 52
sound, link of language to: in early
  views on nature of language, 5–6;
  persistence of view, 6. *See also*
  sensorimotor interface
Spanish Civil War, anarcho-
  syndicalism of, xxi, 63
Squire, Larry, 95
standards, universally applied, as
  concept universally supported
  and everywhere violated, 60
Stapp, H. P., 124
state: control of, by corporate
  interests, xxiii; as iron cage,
  xxiii, 67; oppressive, anarchist
  opposition to, 67–68; as protector
  of oppressed against ravages of
  capitalism, xxiii, 67
Stoljar, Daniel, 91, 101, 113–14, 121–24,
  127
Strawson, Galen, 31–32, 113–16,
  120–21, 124, 127
Strawson, Peter, 43

strong generation, definition of, 4
strong minimalist thesis (SMT),
  24–25
subjectivist revolution, 51

Tattersall, Ian, 3, 7–8, 25, 40
Thackray, Arnold, 107, 113
theoretical linguistics, tentative
  nature of progress in, vii
theory of language, as necessarily a
  generative grammar, ix, 4
theory of mind, 105–6; pragmatic
  approach to, 105–6, 117
Thiel, Udo, 37, 46, 51
thing, as term, identity conditions
  for, 49–50
thinking matter: Locke on possibility
  of, 34–35, 83–84, 113, 114; Priestley
  on, 111–13
thought: language as instrument
  of, 13–16, 23; link of language to,
  7–8, 129n1; as most frequent use
  of language, 14. *See also* computational procedure; conceptual-
  intentional interface
  CONSCIOUS: danger of restricting
    investigation to, xvii; as fragment
    of inner language use, xvii, 14,
    38–39, 59
  IDENTIFICATION OF, WITH CON-
    SCIOUSNESS, 37–38; and conscious
    thought as fragment of subcon-
    scious activity, xvii, 14, 38–39, 59;
    and science of mind, 39

will, as ongoing philosophical problem, 94–95
women, exclusion of from U.S. personhood, 46, 47
Word and Object (Quine), 21, 42
Words and Things (Brown), 42
words or lexical items, atomic elements of computation as prior to, xviii, 41

workers, subordination of: and American libertarianism, 66; history of U.S. activism against, 72–75

Yablo, Stephen, 119
Yolton, John, 113, 114

Zeki, Semir, 96